www.triggerpublishing.com

Thank you for purchasing this book.
You are making an incredible difference.

Proceeds from all Trigger books go directly to
The Shaw Mind Foundation, a global charity that focuses
entirely on mental health. To find out more about
The Shaw Mind Foundation visit,
www.shawmindfoundation.org

MISSION STATEMENT

Our goal is to make help and support available for every
single person in society, from all walks of life.
We will never stop offering hope. These are our promises.

Trigger and The Shaw Mind Foundation

Dad, Mum and Natalie,
Thank you for being there for me
I love you with all my heart.

Disclaimer: Some names and identifying details have been changed to protect the privacy of individuals.

Trigger encourages diversity and different viewpoints, and is dedicated to telling genuine stories of people's experiences of mental health issues. However, all views, thoughts, and opinions expressed in this book are the author's own, and are not necessarily representative of Trigger as an organisation.

The voice of mental health

The**inspirational**series™
Overcoming adversity and thriving

Running with Robins
BEREAVED, NOT BROKEN

BY GEMMA BELL

We are proud to introduce The**inspirational**series™. Part of the Trigger family of innovative mental health books, The**inspirational**series™ tells the stories of the people who have battled and beaten mental health issues. For more information visit: www.triggerpublishing.com

THE AUTHOR

Gemma Bell runs to celebrate being alive. She recently ran a marathon in memory of her dad, and raised over £2500 for Cancer Research UK. Following her own experiences, she is keen to help others recognise the wealth of physical and mental benefits of running, but also the dangers.

Gemma enjoys a wide range of activities as well as running, including horse riding, cooking and spending time with her family.

First published in Great Britain 2018 by Trigger

Trigger is a trading style of Shaw Callaghan Ltd & Shaw Callaghan 23 USA, INC.

The Foundation Centre

Navigation House, 48 Millgate, Newark

Nottinghamshire NG24 4TS UK

www.triggerpublishing.com

British Library Cataloguing in Publication Data

A CIP catalogue record for this book is available upon request
from the British Library

ISBN: 978-1-911246-89-3

This book is also available in the following e-Book formats:

MOBI: 978-1-911246-92-3
EPUB: 978-1-911246-90-9
PDF: 978-1-911246-91-6
AUDIO: 978-1-789560-05-3

Gemma Bell has asserted her right under the Copyright,

Desi   s work

A.

CHAPTER 1

Cherished Childhood

Curling up on the sofa and re-watching some of my dad's old camcorder videos of my family never fails to make me smile and laugh. One of my favourite tapes is of me with my twin sister, Natalie, when we were five years old, in our first ballet performance of *Snow White*. We were skipping around on stage in our homemade bluebird costumes. I can remember Mum spending hours every evening for two weeks sewing scraps of blue material together to make our wings, and attaching them to our turquoise gym leotards. Dad used his artistic skills to create birds' heads and beaks, using the cardboard from cereal boxes and painting them royal blue. He then stapled strips of elastic to go under our chins so that they didn't fall off as we pranced about.

Seeing us fluttering about in our lovingly made costumes with the other girls dressed as woodland creatures fills me with joy. I still get tingles down my spine, just as I had done while waiting backstage at the show. As soon as I had made my entrance, I spotted Dad in the middle of the auditorium with his trusty camcorder, giving me a huge "thumbs up". I smiled at the camera and resisted waving until the end.

With a passion for photography and filming, Dad bought that camcorder to capture all our precious times together.

I'm incredibly grateful to have all these family videos; they remind me of how lucky I was to have had such a wonderful childhood. We were a very small, close-knit family. Dad was like an old-fashioned Englishman – tall and lanky with light-brown hair, freckles and glasses. Mum is Chinese, very petite with dark hair and a round, kind face. Both of them worked full-time so the weekends were the only time we had all together.

Sundays were my favourite day of the week because late morning we'd gather in the living room for elevenses. Natalie and I would raid the tin for the best biscuits, before Mum and Dad had a chance. Sitting back in my squishy beanbag with a handful of dark chocolate Digestives and hot Ribena was the best way to start Sunday.

Once we'd finished scoffing our biscuits, Dad would usually suggest a bike ride or rollerblading. Our bike rides around the woods were the highlight of the weekend for me. Racing Dad on my purple Raleigh bike and whizzing up and down the hills was so exhilarating. Nothing else mattered, apart from trying to catch up with Dad. I never did though, and that just spurred me on to pedal even faster.

I had boundless energy, and was happiest playing outside and letting my imagination run wild. I grew up being very competitive, partly because of being an identical twin. We may have looked the same to most people, but Mum and Dad saw us as complete individuals and treated us that way. They never referred to us as "the twins" or dressed us the same. We have different personalities; I'm older by two minutes and have always been the dominant one.

There was an intense rivalry between us, which would frequently result in shouting and kicking matches. Our sisterly squabbles were often over petty things like who would sit in the front car seat. In my mind, being the eldest – even if it was only by two minutes – meant it was my prerogative to win our arguments and be right the whole time. Dad was always the patient mediator who would resolve the situation, and normally, within five minutes, Natalie and I would be happily playing again.

My sporty streak came from Dad who was very fit and active. Every day, he was up at the crack of dawn to go for a quick run before helping with the school run. I could completely depend on Dad; he was very organised and punctual with everything. We were never late with him. It was often a last-minute rush with Mum, but I knew she'd usually be waiting for us in the car park at home time. I couldn't wait to finish school and tell her about my day. I looked forward to the car ride home because without fail Mum would bring a yummy snack and cartons of apple juice for us to enjoy.

From the age of four, Dad took me to swimming, ballet and gymnastics classes which I loved. He would stay to watch the lessons, so I always wanted to impress him. He wasn't a bullish parent who pressurised me to win, but was keen for me to improve and reach my full potential. No matter how well I had performed, Dad would cheerily greet me at the end of the lesson and give me a huge hug. I loved how reassuring and comforting that was. It motivated me to do better the next week.

I was building up a large collection of certificates from all my sports classes, so Dad bought me a glittery silver file to store them all in. I treasure it and still add to it now with my latest achievements, despite it being completely crammed to the point of bursting. Each time I flick through the pages, I'm overwhelmed with countless memories of triumphs – and all those times with my Dad. It reminds me of how far I've come in life, and gives me the boost I sometimes need to keep on striving.

While Dad would be chauffeuring Natalie and me around to all our hobbies, Mum would take care of the domestic things. She was normally bustling in the kitchen, which was like a steam-room with her ancient rice cooker constantly bubbling away producing the fluffiest rice. Her chicken and vegetable stir fries were like warm hugs in a bowl, but her signature dish was her "special fried rice" with authentic Chinese Char Sui pork which she did on special occasions.

Dad wasn't a great cook, but he was excellent with eggs, and taught me how to flip an omelette successfully. Natalie and I enjoyed baking cupcakes on the weekends with Dad – even though most of it was from bought cake mix packets, so we couldn't go wrong. I liked making *Tom and Jerry* cartoon cupcakes which was messy, but Dad didn't mind, and he let us lick the raw cake batter off the spoon once we'd finished. Once the sponges were baked, he'd help us ice them artistically, add edible character stickers and sprinkles before we devoured them all.

I used to dread Sunday evenings because of the thought of school in the morning, but Dad made things easier. He was the early bird who got everything organised. Still half asleep, I'd slowly drift into the bathroom to find my uniform warming up on the radiator, and my Weetabix ready for me in the kitchen downstairs. Meanwhile, Mum was busy overfilling our Disney lunch boxes. They were like mini picnics with tuna mayo sandwiches, sausage rolls, Mr Kipling's cakes, KitKats, satsumas, apples, juice cartons … We were very popular at lunchtime with our friends!

I went to a very small, quaint, independent day school for girls. There were just nine of us in my class including myself and Natalie, so everyone got on together. I wasn't the brightest bulb in the chandelier, but I worked hard and was very creative due to Dad's influence. Art was my favourite subject in school and I tried to get extra marks for all my other work by adding illustrations in the margins. My teacher would compliment me on the pictures, but unfortunately they didn't increase my grades! Creative writing was also an area in which I shone; Natalie and I used to create fairy-tale stories all the time. On rainy days we'd make dens in the house, using the clothes airer and bedsheets, and hide in there, coming up with fun adventures.

We were conscientious students and liked to get our weekly homework done and dusted on a Friday night. We'd sit at the kitchen table, with all our work books and Pocahontas pencil cases sprawled out in front us. And if we didn't understand something, we'd always turn to Dad because he was so bright – and so patient! He rarely lost his temper, even when we asked him to explain fractions for the hundredth time on a Friday night.

Teachers would find it impossible to tell us apart in school, so they asked Mum to sew a 'G' and an 'N' onto our cardigans to help them avoid mixing us up. But of course, that was completely pointless – Natalie and I would just swap cardigans, or swap seats, to confuse the teacher, and it would have the whole class in stitches.

I excelled in sports and was on the school netball and swimming teams. Mum and Dad never missed a match. One of them would be there to cheer me on and hug me at the end. The annual summer Sports Day was the only time they both came. Dad would be poised with his camcorder to capture my races which gave me more determination to win. I was a sore loser, but having the support of Mum and Dad, win or lose, meant I didn't stay moody for long.

I liked school but couldn't wait for the Christmas holidays – my favourite time of the year. The sparkle of Christmas has never faded. Even as I've got older, it's kept its magic. As soon as I receive my chocolate advent calendar from Mum at the end of November, I'm transported back to when I was a little girl again.

Like most families, we have Christmas traditions which haven't changed in decades. The day would begin with Natalie and me bursting into Mum and Dad's room at 5.00am squealing with excitement that Father Christmas had been, and wanting to open our stockings on their bed. Mum would be hiding under the covers trying to go back to sleep, but Dad leapt up and joined in with our excitement.

If I was a Tomboy the rest of the year, I wanted to be a Disney Princess on Christmas day. I had a huge selection of party dresses, lacy tights, and pearl headbands, which I adored wearing.

Dad would twirl me around the kitchen, so that all the petticoats would float around me, making me feel very regal. And he would keep us all entertained by singing along to Christmassy songs.

We'd all be merry and silly. I didn't like the cracker bangs, so Dad would remove them, and as we pulled them, he would yell 'BANG' which made me giggle and jump in my chair. In the afternoon we'd play with our new toys, and enjoy a refreshing walk, before we'd all sit down to watch *The Snowman*, which still brings tears to my eyes.

One year, my paternal nanny knitted me a robin toy for Christmas and I began the tradition of buying a new robin decoration for the Christmas tree. I have been besotted by robins ever since I was four and I received an RSPB encyclopaedia. The chapter on robins was the first one I flicked to, and I would recite it to Dad every night, when I was tucked up in bed. Those festive family traditions were important to us because we spent quality time together.

I used to really look forward to the Easter holidays as well because we'd always spend a long weekend in Bournemouth. We'd stay in the same hotel and Dad would make sure Natalie and I had our own room with bunkbeds. We'd spends hours playing on the beds, pretending we were on a pirate's ship. Most mornings Dad would take us beachcombing before breakfast while Mum would snooze until we came bounding back with our buckets full of shells and other bits and bobs we'd discovered left by the tide. My favourite time of day though was late afternoon when we gathered together on my parents' bed, munching crisps and drinking lemonade while playing card games like Snap. I treasured these times.

Our big family holiday was in August. Mum and Dad would keep the destination a surprise so it was thrilling waking up in the early hours finding out the destination. The most memorable one was our holiday to the USA when I was nine years old. It was a three-week road trip along the East Coast stopping off at

Hollywood and all the major tourist attractions. Seeing a killer whale in SeaWorld, San Diego was a dream come true. I'd been obsessed with killer whales since seeing the *Free Willy* film, and I was captivated by the magnificent creatures as they effortlessly leapt in the pools.

At Disneyland, I bought a huge Dumbo elephant cuddly toy that was almost larger than me. It was a bit of a struggle bringing him home though, because he was too large to fit in the overhead lockers on the plane. In the end, I had to have him seat-belted to my lap for the long flight. Natalie was sat next to me with a huge Winne-the-Pooh toy on her lap; we got some funny looks from the other passengers!

Landing at Heathrow in the pouring rain was a bit depressing. But as soon as the taxi dropped us off home, I couldn't wait for one of Mum's comforting Chinese meals, and we'd pester Dad to get the camcorder set up. As a treat, Mum would let us eat our warming wonton noodles in the living room, and we'd laugh at ourselves on the videos. It was the ideal way to cheer us all up, and relive the special times we'd had on holiday.

The only time I didn't want to return to school was the first day of senior school. It was such a large school – especially compared to our old primary school – and the academic standards were very high, so I was feeling very apprehensive about it. I was physically shaking as I attempted to tie my new tartan tie over my deep yellow shirt. Dad had to help me do it in the end. I rolled up the very heavy, itchy kilt several times because it was far too long. My new patent shoes squeaked as I walked, and the navy blazer completely engulfed me. I just wanted to crawl back into bed. But as usual, Dad was reassuring and convinced us that it would be fine because all the other girls in Year 7 would be feeling the same.

Dad played Classic FM on the school run to help calm our anxieties. I liked listening to the people's requests because they were often famous film scores. Suddenly I heard the presenter announce, 'And now a message for Gemma and Natalie on their way to their new senior school ... your mum and dad wish you lots of luck and love today, and would like us to play a piece from *The Nutcracker* ballet ...'

At first I was too shocked to say anything and then I began jumping up and down in the backseat with Natalie. I couldn't believe Mum and Dad had actually emailed in a request for us on national radio. He was laughing as Natalie and I swayed our arms balletically, and hummed to the music, full of glee. Now we felt much more at ease, and confident. I was beaming as Dad hugged me at the drop-off point, and strode into my new classroom. I couldn't wait to tell my classmates that we'd been mentioned on the radio. Just what I needed for the start of a new term in a new school.

For the first time in our school lives, Natalie and I were separated into different form groups, to encourage us to be more independent and help us make new friends. It didn't work. As soon as the break-bell rang we met up by the Year 7 lockers to talk over our first few lessons.

I wanted to work hard and impress the teachers, but at the same I wanted to act "cool" and fit in with the rest of my classmates. I didn't want to be perceived as "teacher's pet" but I'd never been disruptive like some of the girls in my form group.

Some girls were issued with warnings within the first week. Three warnings resulted in detention, or a letter home to your parents. I was determined to avoid getting any warnings throughout my time at the school. I couldn't imagine how shameful it would be to get one and having to tell Mum and Dad. I knew they were pouring a lot of their hard-earnt money into my education, so I didn't want to disappoint them.

A lot of the girls came from wealthy families. Initially I found it intimidating as gleaming Rolls Royces and Bentleys glided down the long drive every morning and afternoon when the girls were dropped off and collected. Neither of my parents had been privately educated, so it was an alien environment for us. Mum drove an old VW Golf which I liked because the backseats had become soft and squishy over the 12 years we'd had it.

As Mum pulled up to collect us during the first week, a snooty, smug girl asked, 'Why does your car have a plastic electric fan on the dashboard? Doesn't it have air-con?' My cheeks went pink, but I wasn't going to let her belittle us. 'No, it doesn't come with air-con because it's a vintage car. Air-con hadn't been invented when it was built. Besides, isn't that what windows are for?' I walked towards Mum's car with my head high, and Mum hugged me for standing up for myself.

Not all the girls were as rude, and I found being in this school made me more determined and competitive. I relished any chance to take part in sports and was chuffed to make the netball, gymnastics and swimming teams.

Within a few weeks I was nominated as swimming captain by my coach. I was over the moon because I'd beaten all the other swimmers – many of them swam for external clubs. Some of the girls doubted my ability to lead them to victory, but I proved them wrong. We never lost a single gala against any of the local schools, and at the end of the year, I was even awarded the swimming trophy.

Mum would always be at every sports contest to cheer me on. The one occasion when she wasn't there was my first netball tournament, and we nearly came last. Mum was like my lucky mascot, so when she wasn't there, I felt like I didn't perform my best. I cried that evening, but Dad made me realise that winning isn't everything. He taught me that losing just gives you the chance to improve. Deep down I knew he was right, so I just had to get over it. Mum wasn't to blame for our defeat. It was a team effort, and I knew it meant we just had to work harder and concentrate on the next match.

Apart from sports I was happiest in art lessons. The huge department room was overflowing with every kind of arty accessory you could imagine. We had an eccentric teacher with spikey, silver / white hair, who wore clashing-coloured clothes, and had a megaphone voice. She was in her late sixties, but had more energy than a Duracell bunny, as she leapt around the classroom, getting us all energised to express our inner Picasso. Her classes were always amusing, and I could relax in my own creative bubble.

I'd begun drawing and painting long before I could read or write. Art was in my blood. I think my creative flare came from Dad who was an excellent draughtsman. Each year he would surprise us with exquisite hand-drawn Christmas and birthday cards, usually a Disney character. The best one for me was when he drew "Happy" the dwarf from *Snow White*. I attempted to follow in his footsteps by creating my own too, although mine were more a bit more freestyle, with far too much glitter and sequins!

Christmas at school was fun because there were lots of inter-house competitions towards the end of term including swimming, drama and singing. There were four houses – blue, red, yellow and green. I was obsessed with Harry Potter at the time so when I was put into the blue house, I pretended I was in Ravenclaw, while Natalie was in the Red house, which was Gryffindor. Naturally, I wanted my house to win but I'd always want Natalie's to do well too, because I hated seeing her lose. Luckily, our houses finished 1st and 2nd most of the time, so we didn't hold grudges much.

On the last day of term, everyone gathered in the Great Hall, which was decked out in paperchains and wreaths made by students, for a festive lunch. We sang carols and pulled crackers with the teachers, and there was a hum of excitement for the surprise staff panto. It was hilarious seeing our teachers dressed in drag and acting silly. It was the best way to end my first term there.

Once we returned in January, the rest of the academic year seemed to fly by. The only downside to summer was the end of year exams. But I revised hard and passed everything with good grades.

Sports-wise, tennis and rounders were not my cup of tea, and I was useless at the field events in athletics too. The only areas I shone in were the 100m sprint and hurdles, because I was quick and nimble. I was dreading the compulsory 1500m run around the grass track because it was so boring and seemed never-ending. I just about survived and collapsed with a stitch at the end. No way was I ever running that far, ever again!

The annual Sports Day was a highlight though. It felt like a Quidditch match, as all four houses marched onto the pitch wearing their house colours and face paint, all raring to go into battle.

Parents were welcome to come and watch, and I instantly spotted Mum waving and Dad filming in the crowd. I wasn't going to let them or my house down. I flew across the finish line in first place in both my races, and heard a great roar from my team. Nothing beat that feeling of winning.

CHAPTER 2

The Diagnosis

On my thirteenth birthday, Natalie and I had a joint party with our friends as usual. This time we opted for bowling followed by dinner at a pizza restaurant. For the first time, Mum and Dad didn't supervise us so I felt like a "proper" teenager as they dropped us off outside the venue and let us organise things. They reappeared at the end of the meal, to surprise us with two enormous cakes, and somehow got the whole restaurant singing 'Happy Birthday', which was very embarrassing.

Apart from getting the normal adolescent stresses like spots and greasy hair, I had to get braces. Not only did I need hideous "train-track" braces for two years, I also had to wear a headbrace every night, for six months, to sort out my overbite. I sobbed through the procedure, while Mum held my hand. I was in agony for days and could only sleep on my back because of the metal contraption sticking out the sides of my head. The following months passed slowly, but I couldn't say it hadn't been worth it when I saw the results.

Mum did try to make the orthodontist appointments enjoyable though. She'd collect me during lunchbreak and after I'd had the braces tightened, she'd buy freshly baked sausage rolls from the bakery for a special treat. We'd munch on them together in the car, chatting, before she dropped me back for afternoon lessons.

The day they finally removed the braces, I felt like a model from a toothpaste advert when I entered the classroom, flashing my perfect smile!

The pressure at school was building. We were starting to prepare for exams. For the first time, I began to feel the pressure to succeed academically; these exams really mattered. I couldn't turn to Dad for help with homework any more because the syllabus was too advanced, so I had to knuckle down and work my socks off to attain good results.

I wasn't unrealistic about my chances, and I didn't expect to get the highest grades, because I wasn't as intelligent as some of the people in my year. But I was aiming to be above average. Most of all, I didn't want to disappoint my parents. I was determined to show that sending me to a private school was worth it.

It was challenging trying to focus on boosting my grades, while staying on top of all my other commitments like piano and violin exams, ballet and gymnastics. Most nights I had a netball or swimming match which delayed getting home for homework and dinner. Things began to get quite stressful, especially because Dad wasn't being his normal, positive self ...

He was quieter than usual, and that enormous reserve of energy that had always kept him going seemed to have deserted him. He didn't complain, but Mum told us he wasn't sleeping much because of headaches and pains in his spine. I was worried. Dad had always been so fit and healthy. I had never seen him even a little bit unwell.

When I saw him swallowing a lot of painkillers one evening, I knew something must be wrong; we all knew how much he hated taking medication. I was afraid to ask him why he was feeling so ill because I was scared of the truth. I hoped that he was just tired or jetlagged from an overseas work trip. I thought he'd be fine within a few days. But he wasn't.

Two weeks passed slowly, and we could all see that Dad was getting worse. He couldn't lie down because his back hurt too much. He was restless. He'd lost his appetite. He stopped going for runs. Yet he still refused to go to the doctors. Desperate to know what was wrong, I gently asked him why he wouldn't see a doctor, and he just told me was "fine" and he'd be back to his old self soon.

I didn't believe him, but I didn't want to argue. I wanted to help, but he kept brushing aside any assistance we offered him. I knew he wanted to put on a brave face for us all, but I feared his stubbornness was making him worse.

So I asked Mum what was wrong. Just like Dad had done, she tried to reassure me that he'd be fine. But I knew she was hiding her anxiety when she didn't make eye contact with me, and then swiftly changed the subject. I sensed I wasn't going to get any more out of my parents, so I stopped antagonising them. That just left me fretting even more. I tried to block out whatever was happening and concentrate on my school work.

Dad didn't take any time off work, and kept on doing the morning school run, so our family routine stayed pretty much the same. But I noticed he was much thinner as he got out of the car when dropping us off. His trousers and shirt were baggier on him, and when he kissed me goodbye, I saw his face was pale. He looked worried.

One evening he cried out in agony as he tried to climb the stairs on all fours. The pain was so bad, he couldn't get upstairs any other way. I choked when I heard him. I had never seen Dad like this. He was so strong and fit. Why couldn't he shake off whatever illness he had? Mum had to help him into an armchair in the living room to rest. It was no good. Nothing helped.

In the morning, Mum made an emergency doctor's appointment and drove him there. Dad was immediately transferred to a private hospital near us for further examinations to identify the cause of the pain.

I was slightly relieved. With Dad in hospital, I was confident they'd be able to cure him. He'd be himself, and home again in no time.

But Dad didn't come home. Three weeks passed and the specialists still couldn't find out exactly what was wrong. They gave him strong drugs to ease the pain, but that was it.

Mum brought Natalie and I to visit Dad every day after school. I had never been to a hospital before, and I felt like I was entering a church or a library. I felt compelled to speak in a whisper, afraid of making a noise or being a nuisance.

Seeing Dad all alone in his room broke my heart. I'd never seen him like this. He looked so weak and frail lying on his airbed with a drip attached to him. When he stood up to hug us goodbye, I noticed he looked shorter. His spine was beginning to curve at the top like an elderly person. I didn't say anything because I didn't want to hurt his feelings. I asked Mum about it in the car on the way home and she didn't know why it was happening either.

I made Dad a Get Well card and tried to remain in good spirits when I saw him chatting about my school day and told him silly jokes. My heart sank though when Dad didn't laugh. His sense of humour seemed to have evaporated.

I hated him being away from home for so long. Our routine changed, and I felt disorientated. Mum had to take care of everything. She didn't show her emotions much, and I could feel the silence as she tried to bottle her feelings in, as if she was determined not to show any sign of weakness. You could see that she was working hard to put on a brave face. Like a swan, she was calm and composed on the surface, but fighting furiously against the tide underneath.

Mum was under an immense amount of pressure trying to keep everything under control without Dad's support. Not only did she have a full-time job, but she also had the household to run, shopping to do, and she was visiting Dad in hospital every day. I couldn't have done what she did.

I tried not to worry about Dad too much because I knew there wasn't anything I could do. I knew he was receiving the best possible care, but I felt awful waiting and hoping, and never knowing what was going to happen next.

We were in limbo. Why didn't the doctors know the cause of his illness so they could treat him?

It took six weeks of examinations to find out the answer. I can remember the precise moment when Mum told us the diagnosis. We were in our living room, sitting on the sofa. Mum took our hands in hers and said simply, 'Girls, Dad has cancer.'

There was a long silence. I hoped I'd misheard her. But then Mum's eyes began to well up and she wrapped both arms around us tightly.

It couldn't be true. Dad was too young. He was healthy, he didn't drink, he didn't smoke. Cancer was something old people got.

'Are you sure, Mum? Are the doctors right?'

Mum tried to hold back her tears, but couldn't say anything.

Eventually she let us go and managed to explain, 'He's got a rare bone marrow cancer called multiple myeloma. The myeloma cells divide and expand within the bone marrow, damaging the bones and affecting the production of healthy blood cells. It usually affects the spine, ribs and pelvis. That's why Dad has such bad back pain.'

'Okay, but how are they going to cure it? How long will he be in hospital for?'

'Sweethearts, I really don't know. The doctors are going to try all they can to make him well. Dad is going to be very brave and have all the treatment possible to stop it spreading.'

The word "cancer" echoed in my head all day and night. I didn't know anyone who had cancer, and I didn't think I'd heard of anyone who'd survived cancer. How long would it be until Dad got well and managed to get rid of it?

I felt cold inside as I suddenly remembered watching Disney's *The Lion King*, when Simba had to see his dad dying when he was only little. I was eight years old when I saw the movie, and I'd cried in Dad's arms. He squeezed me tightly and told me it wasn't real; nothing like that would ever happen in our family. I couldn't stand seeing Simba losing his father like that. And I couldn't imagine what I'd do if I ever lost either of my parents.

I knew there would be a happy ending, but I was still so scared of my parents dying. How would I cope without them? I didn't want to think about death, it was too overwhelming, and I'd avoided watching Bambi or *The Lion King* again.

But now, at 13 years old, all those old fears resurfaced. Dad had cancer. I felt the panic rising inside me. How would we cope as a family? What was going to change?

I tried to calm down. Perhaps I was overreacting? Maybe it wasn't that serious, and I was getting worked up unnecessarily?

We did our best to carry on as normal after Dad's diagnosis. I didn't tell my friends at first, because I didn't want it to be true. I thought that by keeping it to myself and not saying the words 'Dad has cancer' out loud, it might make it go away.

But in the end, I had to tell my closet friends because I needed to accept the fact that I couldn't sweep it under the carpet any more. It wouldn't disappear if I ignored it. I also didn't want rumours to start going around, and I really didn't want people to stare at Dad if they saw him looking so pale and thin.

Most of my friends were just as shocked as me. But they seemed more concerned about how Dad was, than how I was feeling. So, I kept a brave face at school. I wanted to appear strong and optimistic even though I had no idea if Dad was getting better. When I asked him or Mum about what was happening, they were always vague. I didn't probe further. Ignorance helped me carry on. I tried not to dwell on it.

Dad was stable enough to come home by Halloween, and his company sent him some projects to do at home, so he could stay occupied and maintain a routine. It was reassuring to have Dad back home with us. He started doing the school run again, and took us to ballet and gymnastics, just as he'd always done.

By Christmas he seemed perkier. The drugs he was on were obviously helping. As usual, Natalie and I were up at dawn to open our stockings and play games. Dad joined in with us by singing Christmas songs. The day was full of cheer, and it felt like Dad was himself again. The only difference was that he became tired easily and went to bed early, while the rest of us stayed up to watch *White Christmas*. I didn't mind as long as he had enjoyed himself. I think he had.

Dad began attending our local hospice on Wednesdays to get some respite care. To me, it felt like a bright, welcoming place. The homely communal area was full of armchairs and sofas, and the staff were so friendly and sympathetic. I know now that it was a haven for people with terminal illnesses. But at the time, I didn't know that.

There were therapies to help Dad relax, and even a dedicated art room. This was his favourite place. He'd spend the whole day creating something like a water-colour painting and return home, proudly showing it to us. Now our house is adorned with art which reminds me of him.

By the summer, Dad was well enough to fly, so we booked a family holiday to Malta. It wasn't a long holiday because we didn't want to risk Dad being away from medical support, but being away together really boosted all our spirits.

As a special treat, Mum and Dad arranged for us to swim with dolphins. It must have been top of our wish list ever since we'd been very little. The experience was beyond what I had imagined. I can still remember the feel of the dolphins' rubbery skin, and the sheer exhilaration of being pulled along, while I held on to a dorsal fin. Dad recorded it all (of course) and I still get tingles watching it back.

The holiday really revitalised us all. For the rest of the year, it seemed as if Dad's cancer was under control. I understood now that Dad was never going to get his height back and that he would remain hunched over, but that didn't matter. All I cared about was that he kept on getting better.

CHAPTER 3

Dad Deteriorates

Entering Year 10 was a massive leap because it marked the beginning of GCSE exams. I chose to do exams in Spanish, French, Geography, Art and RE, to accompany the compulsory Double Science, Double English and Maths. Studying suddenly became more interesting because I was doing subjects I shone in and really enjoyed.

I still continued with my ballet, gymnastics, netball and swimming, but I gave up the violin and piano lessons, because it was all a bit too much to focus on.

Dad was constantly in and out hospital, trying different treatments. The cancer was getting more aggressive, and we were desperately hoping for a way to stop it spreading so rapidly.

First, he tried radiotherapy, followed by chemotherapy. I didn't know what either of them entailed, or even how they would affect Dad. Whenever I asked, I was only ever given very basic explanations. I just assumed the therapies would kill off all the bad cells in his body, without leaving any obvious visible signs. I was wrong.

When Dad opened the front door one afternoon, after his chemo session, I screamed out, not recognising him. He was completely bald! Nobody warned me that he was going to lose his hair! He reassured me that it was him by making a joke out his dramatic change in appearance. 'Like my new style?' he said, imitating a catwalk model pose.

I was lost for words. I had no idea what to say without offending him.

'Did it hurt?' was I all managed to say. 'Not at all, it just all fell out overnight. At least it makes showering quicker!' he replied, trying to stay upbeat.

I giggled and began to feel more at ease. If I'd lost all my hair I'd refuse to go out, but he remained undeterred. He didn't care how he looked, or what people thought any more. He simply wore a farmer's cap when we went out, and ignored people's stares. I wished I had his self-confidence.

By the summer of 2004, Dad had to give up work completely because his hands shook too much to draw or write. Watching him struggle with the most basic tasks was heart-wrenching. I offered to help, but he refused and shouted at me. I knew he didn't mean to yell, but I was still hurt – and just a little bit annoyed by his stubbornness.

The consultants recommended he have a stem-cell transplant in Hammersmith Hospital, London. That meant Dad had to be completely isolated for six weeks. At first, I didn't understand why he had to be completely shut off from the world for so long, but they told me he would have no immune system. He would be especially susceptible to infections until his healthy white cells began to multiply again.

I didn't want him to go, but if there was the slightest chance it could eliminate the cancer and prevent him from getting worse, we didn't have a choice. It was hard on Mum. Every day, she made the long drive to visit Dad. She would come back to look after Natalie and me, and then she had to work in the evenings. She was getting more and more worn out.

At weekends, Natalie and I were allowed to see Dad. Each time I walked along the hospital corridor it felt like I was entering a nuclear bunker. We wore plastic overalls and face masks, and we had to sterilise our hands frequently to kill any germs. I was afraid of going near Dad because I didn't want to risk infecting him. It was heart-breaking; I couldn't even hold his hand or hug him before I left to show how much I loved him.

With only a single window looking out onto the car park below, it felt like prison. I couldn't have endured it. I'd have given up completely in the claustrophobic conditions, and would have been bored to death. I tried to be positive in front of him though, and held back the tears until I got to the car.

But Dad soldiered on through two stem-cell transplants over two years.

Mum kept his spirit alive by giving him things to look forward to. She was determined to have our annual summer holiday abroad together, so she booked a short vacation to Menorca, which was very relaxing. Dad did perk up being so near the sea, in the warm sunshine. He even taught me to play table tennis so that I could have a match with the Spanish boys in our hotel.

Back home, I was entering Year 11: exam year, and I was feeling the stress of trying to exceed my predicted B grades.

It was also prom year. I'd dreamt of wearing a Disney-style princess gown since I was a little girl. Dad wanted to take us dress shopping instead of Mum! So, he patiently sat on a sofa in a wedding dress shop while Natalie and I fluttered about in sumptuous gowns. We picked very different styles in the end which suited our personalities.

The big day arrived in May, and Dad was in his element, filming every stage of the process, from hair and make-up, to parading outside when the white limo pulled up for us with our friends and boyfriends. It was a typical "chick-flick" moment with our proud parents waving us off.

The prom was our last chance to let our hair down before the exams. Our exams were spread out over several weeks which meant we were allowed to study from home. I made the most of the opportunity to spend more time with Dad. He did his best to help me revise by buying colourful pens for my revision notes, and keeping me company during my study breaks and lunchtime. In the evening, he would offer to take me to the sports club so that I could de-stress with a swim or a gym session. I felt guilty though because I knew how much he used to love going. Now, he could barely walk unaided.

He was very sleepy for most of the day and would snooze in his armchair, or if he had the energy, potter in the garden.

I crammed in as much revision as possible which wasn't easy when I just wanted to be outside in the sunshine. Natalie was going through it all too, so we could moan about it together, and test each other on our subjects. I drew a huge revision timetable and stuck it on my bedroom wall to give me a sense of achievement at the end of the day when I could tick off the subjects. I never felt fully prepared though, and took all my revision cards and books in the car on the way to ensure the information was fresh in my head.

Dad wanted to feel productive and useful so insisted on driving us to every one of our exams, and waited patiently in the car, listening to Radio 4 until we were finished. As always, he was great at lifting my mood when I was convinced I'd failed a paper. He'd say something comical, and touch my arm reassuringly before putting on some music.

The results day was in August, and Dad seemed even more excited than Natalie or me as he drove us to school to collect the envelopes. I opened mine by myself, and couldn't believe I'd got 1 B, 6 As and 3 A* grades, making me one of the highest achievers in the year! Suddenly I was one of brightest bulbs in the chandelier! Seeing Dad so ecstatic was what really made me happy though.

Mum and Dad "pulled out the red carpet" by treating Natalie and me to afternoon tea at the Ritz hotel in London to celebrate. I had tingles down my spine as I entered the grand lobby wearing my posh outfit, and Dad proudly showed off his new suit. I felt like we were having tea in the company of royalty; it was incredibly decadent, especially with the string quartet playing in the background. Sitting together in the Ritz's palatial surroundings made all the hard work worth it, and it's one of my most cherished memories.

I couldn't wait for our summer holiday; we all needed to get away and relax. The change of scenery and bright sunshine certainly lifted our spirits. It was hard to see Dad struggling to lift our luggage because he was so weak. He couldn't sunbathe either, because his skin was too sensitive, and he couldn't go paddling in the sea like he used to. One thing that didn't change though was his appetite for ice cream. Every evening he would always have scoops of vanilla and strawberry with lashings of different sauces and sprinkles, just like he'd always done. His sense of humour didn't waver either, he was brilliant at cracking jokes with the waiters. Just hearing him laugh made me feel so happy. He was more himself on holiday, and I missed that when we were at home.

I tried not to think about the holiday coming to an end; I didn't want Dad to go back into hospital and suffer through more treatment. He had already been through so much, what more could they do? When would he be free of it?

I never asked my parents how long it would go on for. It never really occurred to me that he wouldn't get any better – and I never allowed myself to think that. I just kept on assuming Dad would be strong enough to fight it off.

September arrived, and my stomach was in knots, because Natalie and I would be starting at sixth form college to study for our A levels. We would have liked to have stayed at our old school, but now that Dad wasn't working, we couldn't afford the fees any more. I was devastated at first. I even tried to get the art scholarship to reduce the cost, but it was still too much for my parents.

Beginning sixth form was a massive change. There were nearly 2000 pupils in all; my previous school had just 350! For the first time, I was having to mingle with boys in class sizes of 20. The only time I'd mixed with boys was at the Saturday night school socials during Year 10 and Year 11. We had been escorted by our matron to the boys' school and she'd watched us with hawk eyes, ensuring there was no "funny business". As such, I had barely spoken to boys, let alone had a proper boyfriend.

Within a few weeks, I had settled into my new classes and found my way around the huge complex. The best part was when I was selected for the netball team after several days of tough trials. Dad was there, cheering me on, as he had done throughout my life. He punched the air and patted me on the back when I was picked to be part of the first team. We were both as pleased as punch.

Some of my friends from senior school moved to the same college, and I tended to stick with them at lunchtimes at first. I felt very mature now that I was more in control of my daily routine and had to take responsibility for my actions. Unlike school where I was obliged to stay the whole day for lessons and extra-curricular activities, at college I could choose to go home when I liked and not even go in at all if I had no lessons. It was a taster of what university life would be like.

I liked having the freedom to do as I pleased. I was never tempted to skip classes though because I was so driven to be the best in this bigger establishment. I enjoyed learning and wanted to get good grades to go to university. I didn't share any lessons with Natalie so I developed a new identity and was simply known as "Gem" to my classmates. Most of them didn't believe me when I said I had a twin sister because they never saw me with her. It was very amusing when I showed them a photo of Natalie and me to prove it.

It was interesting meeting girls and guys from different backgrounds. At school I had felt a little out of place because my family wasn't wealthy, but the majority of people at college weren't posh and privileged, just completely normal. I didn't miss my old school as much as I thought I would. Despite my initial reservations about going to college, I began to realise after a few weeks that it was the right choice, not just because of our family financial situation, but also because of the wealth of opportunities on offer. And I soon realised that I enjoyed the challenge.

CHAPTER 4

Losing Dad

I was engrossed with my studies and my new life at college, and happy that Dad was getting the best possible care. He was spending more time in the hospice to give Mum some respite. The medical team were so caring, that I knew he was in safe hands, and they had the facilities to make him more comfortable with automated beds and chairs.

It was only after Christmas, when he caught a cold and couldn't shake it off, that I noticed how much more poorly he seemed; how much frailer. By mid-January, he had got shingles and he was too ill to go out for my birthday meal. I didn't feel like celebrating my seventeenth birthday. It was horrible seeing and hearing him cough and wheeze. It was obvious that he was having trouble breathing, and he was drowsy most of the time because he was on the strongest dosage of drugs.

Mum and Dad generously bought us driving lessons for our birthday. I should have been delighted, but I hated knowing that my dad wouldn't be teaching me. That's what dads do with their teenage children. Instead, Mum insisted on taking me out in her Toyota Corolla before my first lesson, just so that I got a head start. Dad was a calm, safe driver, whereas I'd say Mum was more "freestyle"!

'Stop, Gemma! Just stop! Use the brake pedal! That's the accelerator! You nearly crashed into that trolley! Didn't you see it?! Get out of the car and into the passenger seat, I'm driving you home! I'm never taking you out ever again until you pass your exam!' Mum yelled at me.

'It's not my fault! You didn't explain it to me properly. I hate driving! Dad should've been here with me doing this, not you! I'm never driving your stupid big car again!'

Driving with Mum that night just stressed me out even more. I knew it wasn't her fault, but I decided to postpone my lessons with an instructor. I just couldn't cope, it felt as if it was all getting worse ...

A few days later, Dad yelled, 'Someone please give me a shotgun! I can't take it any more! I can't live life like this! I don't want to go on living.' After that, I couldn't get the image of Dad trying to kill himself out of my mind.

What do you do when your parent wants to die?

Would Dad actually find a way to kill himself?

What could I do to stop him taking his life?

I heard him crying as he retreated to the living room. I went and spoke to him nervously – did he really want to die?

'Yes, sweetheart, I do sometimes wish to die because I am in so much pain, and I look and feel wretched.' I gently put my arm around him (I was scared of touching him and hurting him because I knew his spine was so very tender) and tried to comfort him. He gave a little smile and told me not to worry. 'Of course I'm not going to actually kill myself, but I hate being like this.'

There was nothing I could say to make him well. But I hoped that simply hugging him helped. Those hateful words echoed in my head for days. Dad had never shown his vulnerability until now. He had always put on a brave face and stayed optimistic. But now, I couldn't help thinking the light of his soul was slowly extinguishing.

He was fading fast. I was losing him.

Dad was in and out of the hospice during February, and now he needed 24-hour care. Mum was tearing her hair out, working full-time and running our household, so it helped to know Dad was getting the care he needed. I still clung onto the hope that he'd recuperate and come home stronger after some respite. But I was wrong.

Later that month, Mum called Natalie and me into the living room to tell us something important. My heart was thumping as I sat down on the sofa and held Mum's hand.

'I'm sorry, girls, but it's not good news ... the medical team have confirmed that there are no more treatments available to combat the cancer. I'm afraid it means that ... Dad is going to die soon ... there's nothing else we can do to reduce his pain. It's only going to get worse from now on.'

I couldn't take it in. How could they have done everything possible if he was still so sick? There had to be something else they could do. I couldn't believe her. Surely they could try another stem-cell transplant or stronger drugs? I felt as if I had to do something. I couldn't just let my dad die.

Suddenly, after all the months and years of pretending things would be alright, it felt as if the end had come. No one had ever said how long Dad would have. I'd just assumed that if the doctors hadn't been able to cure him, they would at least have stopped the cancer from spreading so that he could continue life for many more years, albeit hunched over.

How could they let the cancer kill him? Why were they giving in to defeat?

No one had ever told me it was terminal.

Nothing ever beat Dad. He could survive anything. He was the only person I knew I could rely on, no matter what. I needed him to be there for me forever.

My heart was torn in two. Of course I hated seeing Dad suffering so badly, and I wished I could let him go; let him be at peace. He had no enjoyment in life. He didn't have any mobility, and now he was struggling to breathe because his lungs were so compressed by his hunched back. The cancer had corrupted him and torn our family apart.

But I was selfish, and I couldn't – I wouldn't – let go. My world would disintegrate without him. He had always overcome life's problems. He was a fighter. He always soldiered on. That's what I expected him to do! To hear that he had actually given up – that he could no longer fight – was heart-wrenching. 'I don't want to carry on,' he told us. 'The cancer is killing me, I'm scared ...'

There was nothing I could do. I turned to Mum for comfort, pleading with her to do something – anything – to help Dad. She fought back her tears as she told me that they'd agreed not to tell Natalie or me that the cancer was terminal when they'd found out three years ago. They hadn't wanted to scare us. I think it was probably best that I didn't know right from the beginning; I'm not sure I would have coped with knowing. But finding out like that was such a shock. I panicked that I didn't have enough time left with him. Perhaps if I'd been told earlier, I would have felt like I had more time to accept that he was going to die. Perhaps I'd have been able to make every minute I had with him matter.

The doctors had told Mum and Dad that he'd have between six months and three years to live – the fact that he had survived as long as he had was miraculous. But now the consultants confirmed that the cancer had spread to his vital organs ... he didn't have much time left and there was nothing they could do.

With the tears rolling down her cheeks, Mum tried to tell us that it was Dad's choice to let go now. He had no enjoyment left in life. There was only the constant pain ... and the waiting for death. He couldn't go on hiding behind his heroic façade, he couldn't fight any more. He wanted to be at peace.

My mouth went dry and I felt hollow as I tried to take it in. On some level, I understood why they had chosen not to tell us that the cancer was slowly killing him. I had always hoped against hope that he would get better, and now it was almost impossible to let go of that hope.

We hugged each other tightly and Mum said that now he had come to terms with what was going to happen next, Dad wanted to come home. He didn't want to die in the hospice. We all knew it was the right choice. We wanted to be as close to him as possible; we needed to try to make the most of the time we had left with him.

The staff at the hospice were organising his transfer home for the next day, so we spent the rest of the evening tidying and cleaning the house for him to come home. I couldn't believe this was all happening. It didn't feel real. You can clean and make things comfortable, but how do you prepare for your parent to come home to die?

I hated feeling out of control and helpless. I was restless and didn't know what to do. Mum tried to remain calm and strong that evening and we gathered in the living room to watch a silly movie; it didn't help in the slightest. My mind was all-consumed by Dad. I couldn't wait to see him, I didn't want to leave his side.

I didn't sleep at all and was glad to get up for college in the morning. Mum took the day off work to help with Dad being transferred home. I was glad to be outside and among friends. Having a routine and concentrating in class helped to pass the time and meant I didn't think about Dad the whole time.

When I got home that afternoon, my heart sank as I saw all the medical equipment and supplies laid on the hall floor. Dad was in the living room, quietly snoozing in his armchair, exhausted by the journey home.

Everything was a blur, with friends and family all rushing over to see him, and trying to help. By early evening, we were all exhausted. Mum made Dad's favourite childhood tea, which was a cheese sandwich, followed by jelly and ice cream. He didn't have much of an appetite but ate most of his – he seemed to enjoy his final meal with us.

I wasn't hungry. I looked across the table at my dad. He was a completely different man from the vivacious man I had grown up loving. Apart from the dramatic change in his appearance, his personality and sense of humour had evaporated. The cancer had stolen my dad and left us with a quiet invalid. Someone I hardly knew.

Mum had to half-carry him as he attempted to crawl upstairs. I couldn't watch. I waited until she had changed him into his PJs before entering the room.

'Good girls, you were always good girls, help Mum tomorrow,' he croaked before shuffling to his airbed, supported by Mum, and lying down.

I blew him a kiss goodnight and said I'd see him in the morning.

Within a few hours it was clear that he was deteriorating fast. He was disorientated and he could barely remember who we all were.

He was confused, tossing and turning on his airbed and shouting incoherently. I barely slept, I was just so scared.

He flipped between conscious and unconscious states throughout the night. My heart would skip a beat when I saw his head tilt back and his eyes shut. 'Mum! Quick he's not breathing!' But then he would suddenly take an enormous gasp and open his eyes again, blinking at me, totally bewildered. I stared at his crushed chest to make sure I could see his heart beating. I saw it in slow motion. Pump. Pause. Pump. Pause. Pump ...

By 2.00am, Mum was panicking. Dad's behaviour was getting more erratic, so in desperation she called our neighbour, Theresa, who is a nurse, to come and check up on him. She managed to calm him down, at first. But less than an hour later, Dad was gasping and crying out in pain. This time Mum phoned for the emergency doctor.

We all huddled round Dad's bed trying to soothe him, but he was inconsolable. His eyes were horrifyingly bloodshot, as if he was possessed, and he kept reaching out for someone or something. Natalie and I just sat there in our dressing gowns, utterly helpless. I wanted to do something, I hated feeling useless. I couldn't bear watching this happen to my dad.

My pulse was racing, wishing the doctor would arrive to help us, but he didn't.

Mum knelt by Dad's bedside and held his hands tightly, her eyes filled with tears. I had never seen her in hysterics. 'We love you and we're all here for you, honey.' I'm not sure Dad understood, or even heard her words, but he gazed at her with wide eyes, as he lay on his side panting with exhaustion.

A loud gurgling sound came, as if he was being strangled. He drew one more breath and then he froze.

I began to panic. Surely this couldn't be the end!

His eyes were still open, but he didn't blink. His tiny chest was motionless.

'No, honey, please don't leave me. I can't live without you! Please don't go yet!' Mum cried out.

The doctor quietly entered the bedroom what felt like hours later (but was really only minutes). He softly shook his head, and verified there was no pulse.

My mouth was dry, I couldn't speak. I sat there shivering with cold sweat. This was it. This was the moment I had been blocking from my mind for three years.

Dad's battle was over.

He was gone.

We were alone.

There was an eerie silence that sent shivers down my spine. It was unbearable. It was dark and damp outside. Mum stayed with Dad, clutching his hand, and talking to his lifeless body. A while later, she made the call to the undertakers.

I couldn't stand looking at him. The more I looked at his motionless body, the more real it became. He was dead, and he was never coming back. I slumped on a chair in the living room in a daze, too exhausted to do anything.

What should I do now? I didn't know the time, but I was wide awake; I couldn't go back to bed now. I could hear Mum wailing, and I felt even more vulnerable. I felt like a little girl again watching Simba from *The Lion King*. Like him, I had lost my dad, my hero. It was horrible seeing Mum collapse – emotionally and physically. I'd never seen her like this. I didn't know what to say or do to make things better.

Natalie had shut herself off in her bedroom crying on the phone to her boyfriend, so I didn't want to disturb her. I didn't feel like I could turn to anyone for a hug and support. I felt utterly abandoned.

I just wanted to snap out of this hell. I wanted someone to wake me up and tell me it was just a nightmare; that everything was fine. But it wasn't.

The undertakers arrived soon after and carefully carried Dad's body away. At the back of my mind I was tricking myself into believing that, somewhere else on Earth, Dad was somehow alive and well, but at the bottom of my heart I knew he had truly gone.

The next 24 hours were the longest and most surreal I have ever experienced. I could barely speak, let alone eat. I was completely deflated. No energy to do anything.

Later that day, I was the only one capable of picking up the phone to call our closest friends and family to deliver the devastating news. 'Hi, it's Gemma. Um, Dad … Dad's gone … he passed away earlier this morning. I have to go …' was all I managed to stutter. I didn't wait to hear their responses. I simply hung up before bursting into tears.

People drifted in and out our house throughout the day which seemed to go on forever. I lost all sense of time. I didn't even realise it was Saturday. Usually I'd be teaching gymnastics which I always looked forward to. But not today. Nothing could lift my spirits.

I couldn't articulate how I was feeling, not even to Natalie and usually we told each other everything. I felt like a mute, unable to get any of my feelings out.

I couldn't wait for it to be over. I wanted to crawl into bed and hide from it all.

In the evening, we hired a chick-flick to try to take ourselves out of the nothingness we felt. But it just made us more upset. The happy ending just rubbed salt into our wounds. Our lives had been completely torn apart by the loss of Dad.

Sunday was worse. I felt sick the whole time, as if someone had punched me in the stomach. Mum couldn't stop crying. The constant texts and phone calls from people was maddening. I turned my phone off. I couldn't face reality.

Natalie and I took a couple of days off from college to help Mum with the funeral arrangements, but we felt as if we needed to return to our "normal" routine quickly. We had to try to find some sort of stability and focus. Being back in college and channelling my energy into my studies and my hobbies helped the time move a little bit faster.

All my friends were shocked at my choice to come back so soon. 'Didn't your dad die on the weekend?' 'Shouldn't you be at home with your mum?' 'Why aren't you wearing black?'

I knew that Dad wouldn't have wanted me to wear black for him, and he certainly wouldn't have wanted us skulking around the house. His funeral was a week later – that was the only day I wore black.

It felt horribly claustrophobic in our house as family members started arriving early in the morning. Everyone whispered, as if Dad was just sleeping upstairs.

'We're so sorry for your loss, you must be missing him.'

'You're so brave. How are you managing?'

'Is there anything I can do to help?'

'He was so young, he shouldn't have died this way ...'

I ran into my room and hid until it was time to follow his coffin to the crematorium.

I hated being the centre of attention, especially the moment when Natalie and I read out the poem we had written about Dad. I hated public speaking, but I wanted to do that for Dad; to show my love for him.

I didn't cry, I was determined to stay strong until I'd finished reading.

It was when the curtains closed behind his coffin that I got a cold chill down my neck as I sat in the pew clutching on to Mum and Natalie. I imagined Dad being cremated. His limp, disfigured body burning and turning to ash. Now there was no way of getting him back. Both his spirit and body were gone.

I could no longer hold back the tears.

This was really it.

This really was the end.

He was never coming home.

CHAPTER 5

Nowhere to Run

Could my life get any worse?!

I was already stressed enough dealing with a normal 17-year-old's issues, like my hormones and keeping on top of my studies. And now I was trying to deal with losing my dad on top of all that! This wasn't something life could have prepared me for. This wasn't something I could have learnt about in a book. Nothing can prepare you for watching your dad die in agony.

How the hell was I going to live my life without Dad?!

I didn't want things to change. I didn't want to adapt. And I didn't want to accept that he was gone.

I just wanted to cocoon myself in my bed and never get up again. I couldn't face the thought of living life without him. I couldn't stop thinking about all the things he was going to miss out on. I hadn't even had my first boyfriend yet! I couldn't envision myself ever being happy or enjoying myself knowing he wouldn't be there to talk to. To confide in. To celebrate my achievements with.

At 17, I should have felt young and free, but instead I was trapped in this nightmare. I was constantly being reminded of Dad. It was the little everyday things that would choke me as I thought of him. The thing I craved most was to hear his voice again.

I missed his laughing and chuckling. Any time I heard children in the playground shouting out 'Daddy!' with delight in their voices, I felt the pain all over again.

Whenever I heard the hall clock strike 6.00pm, I was almost conditioned to expect to hear Dad arriving home and shouting out, 'Hi, girls, I'm home ...' before laying his briefcase on the stairs and coming into the kitchen to greet us all with kisses.

Even when he was ill, and I could just hear him slowly pottering around the house, I found the sense of him being there comforting. Before entering a room, my mind kept tricking me into believing Dad was sitting in there quietly reading or listening to the radio like he used to. I was desperately searching for any indication that he was still at home; that he hadn't gone. But the truth was, no matter how hard I tried to "find him" and convince myself he was still alive, he wasn't.

Six months after his death, it still felt unbearable. The days went by at a snail's pace. I craved endless distractions to get through them. Silences were deadly to me because they gave my mind time to wander. I would get flashbacks of the final seconds of Dad, looking so helpless, gasping for breath. Those excruciating moments were going round and round in my head. I was haunted by them. They scared me. They drained me emotionally. It was as if an evil dementor has escaped from the Harry Potter books and was stalking me. It sucked all the happiness out of my life. I couldn't run or hide. I couldn't get rid of it.

'Try counselling,' someone suggested. Just the word made me shudder. It prompted images of an old Victorian mental asylum. I wasn't insane. I felt as if my life was already bad enough; I didn't want anything to do with counselling.

None of my friends had lost their parents. While they could sympathise, they couldn't empathise – and that difference was crucial. Being pitied by others was patronising. Even friends distanced themselves from me at first because they didn't know what to say, or how to behave around me. Either they didn't get it, or they just assumed I was fine. But that just made me feel like they didn't care.

I deliberately put on a brave face to convince myself that I was fine – and to stop me from breaking down in tears every five minutes. But concealing my true emotions became more challenging as time went on.

I felt like I was drifting in a strange kind of limbo, where everything around me carried on as usual for everyone else. But because my dad wasn't there, it didn't feel like that to me. I didn't feel as if I was participating in the real world. I felt numb all the time. I wanted to escape and feel alive again.

Although I had said the words 'my dad died from cancer in March ...' to friends, family and teachers, it still hadn't completely sunk in – and I didn't want it to. I didn't want it to be true. My heart was hoping that life would go back to how it was before he left us. I longed for him to return home safe and sound, so that he could hug me again and tell me that he loved me. I was holding on and waiting for something that could never materialise, no matter how much I prayed and daydreamed. I was like Peter Pan, not wanting to leave the security of Neverland. But I knew that sooner or later, I was going to have to become Wendy and grow up.

Whenever the subject of dads came up in conversation, it made me feel even more emotional, and envious of all my friends who still had their dads. Every time people mentioned their dads, I had to choke back the tears. None of them knew how lucky they were to have caring dads in their lives. I wished they would make more of an effort to show their dads how much they loved them, instead of mocking and moaning about them. Now that my dad was gone, I regretted not telling him how much I loved him, no matter what.

One of my best friends was moaning about her dad for the hundredth time because he would only buy her a new car if she passed her AS exams. She said he was blackmailing her.

I couldn't believe she was being so ungrateful and disrespectful towards her own dad. She sounded so rude, so spoilt. My dad would never have needed to bribe me to do well in my exams because I'd only ever wanted to make him proud. With tears streaming down my face, I told her 'I'd do anything in the world to have one more day with my dad, so you should shut up and be more considerate!'

I hurried outside to get some fresh air and tried to calm down. I hated hearing people arguing with their parents. I couldn't bear it. Chloe had been one of my closest friends since we were 11 years old, but she had somehow turned into a self-indulged, careless brat. She didn't even apologise to me or her dad (and still got the car she wanted later that summer). I couldn't believe her outrageous behaviour towards me or her dad. We didn't speak much after that. I didn't care, I didn't want any false friends in my life, but losing a friend like that just made me feel even lonelier.

Home felt so much emptier without Dad's presence. And bedtime was awful. It felt like Mum and Natalie would be sound asleep, while I lay wide awake in my dark bedroom. Thoughts of Dad's final moments battling for his life against the cancer were as fresh as if it had just happened. They swirled around in my head, tormenting me and preventing me from sleeping peacefully.

Even during the day, my thoughts were consumed by him and the pain he suffered. It pierced my heart every time I saw him again in my mind's eye, the cancer strangling him to death.

Was this normal? Was I always going to feel like this? Was this grieving? How long would it last? The questions kept buzzing round my head.

I decided I had to do something in memory of Dad. Months ago, Natalie and I had come up with the idea of organising a student charity fashion show to raise money for our local hospice, and for Cancer Research UK. We had forgotten all about it, but decided it would be a good way to channel our emotions into something positive. So, we decided to go for it and set a date at the end of the AS exams.

I was utterly exhausted by the planning and organising involved. Trying to fit it all in between studying and sports commitments was ridiculous! Most nights I stayed up past 1.00 am. But I wanted this project to be perfect for Dad. Natalie and I did everything ourselves – the hiring of designer clothes, booking the venue, brochure design, selling tickets, choreography, music ... we even modelled a few dresses ourselves.

With help from just Mum and a few friends, we pulled it all together in time for the big day in July. The atmosphere was electric backstage with the 20 students (boys and girls) modelling a dozen popular brands. We had a hilarious compere to announce each collection of clothes, and blasted the best summer chart tunes. The whole auditorium was on its feet cheering and wolf-whistling.

The evening flew by. I was still shivering with excitement as Mum drove us home. We'd raised over £1,200 for the two charities, which was beyond our expectations, so I ended the summer term on a real high. But part of me was dreading the holidays. I felt like it wouldn't be any fun without Dad. Going on our annual two-week holiday was the highlight of the year for us as a family, and Dad had always worked so hard to make it special for us. He had always seemed more excited than any of us when we went away. He was the "free rein" parent who let Natalie and I do what we liked on holiday. He'd join in too, making sure that we were enjoying ourselves. For him, our happiness was always the most important thing.

But not this summer. Or ever again.

I had an insatiable desire to be close to him, so when college finished for the summer I would frequently cycle to his gravestone a few miles away from our house. I enjoyed the ride and always took a small bunch of flowers for him. I still wanted to feel like I was including him in some way, so I would talk aloud as I arranged the bouquet in front of his grave.

Then, I would sit on a plastic carrier bag on the grass next to the grave, wishing and praying that he could come back to us. Most of my chats would result in me welling up and sobbing about how much I missed him. I only ever revealed my true feelings when I was alone with him.

Alone apart from the birds …

Any time I saw a robin, it would make me smile. Robins already felt very special to me, and I liked the feeling that there was a symbolic bond between me and the little birds. It made me think back to those bedtimes with my big book of birds, and helped me feel more connected to Dad.

I spent hours just sitting, watching and listening to them twitter away in the hedges surrounding the graveyard. I liked to imagine they'd come to keep me company and bring messages from Dad. I know it sounds silly, but it was comforting.

On one occasion, I was reminded of a short chat I'd had with Dad about running. He'd suggested I go for a jog around the block to help me de-stress from my school studies. Initially I pulled an ugly face and rejected the idea; I loathed running. Anything beyond 100m felt mind-numbingly boring, so why on earth would I want to go and run for "fun"?

Dad's passion for running was definitely not one I shared. I almost fell asleep while watching the London Marathon on TV with him every year. But he would be completely engrossed. It had been one of his life's goals to run it himself, and he'd accomplished that goal in 1989, the year I was born.

I was disappointed when he said he'd forgotten where he'd stored his medal; I would have loved to have seen it. But that was his first and last marathon. He gave up running because he said he did enough running around chasing after Natalie and me. It seemed he had a real passion and talent for it though, and it was such a shame he gave it all up.

The worst part is that I never got to see him run, or even go on a run with him. I imagined he'd have been great company and would have made the time fly by. It saddened me to reflect that there were so many questions I should have asked him when I'd had the chance. Even silly little things like, 'What was your favourite route?' and 'What was the furthest distance you ran?'. Now I'll never know.

I'd seen lots of people go out for their Sunday morning jogs, but was never tempted to give it a go until that summer. I rationalised that if so many other people did it – and kept on doing it – there must a good reason why. Surely it couldn't be that difficult? What was the worst that was going to happen if I gave it a shot?

I remember three distinct pieces of advice Dad gave me: firstly that I should invest in good running shoes because they are a runner's "armour" when they head off to battle the pavements. Secondly, never set off too fast: start slowly at the beginning of a run so that you don't run out of energy. Finally, it was vital to refuel properly after a run, which didn't mean simply gorging on chocolate cake and biscuits.

My dad's favourite post-run meal was a brown bread sandwich with peanut butter and sliced banana inside. What a revolting combination! No way was I eating that. But he patiently explained that was a balanced, wholesome meal consisting of the right amounts of carbohydrates, protein, fat and fibre. My knowledge of running nutrition was zero, but I still wasn't swayed to try his weird sandwich.

Dad was rarely wrong about anything, so I didn't completely discard his suggestion to try running to make myself feel better. After all, what was the worst that could happen?

The morning of my first ever run later that summer, I spent ages fretting about what to wear. Being a typical, self-conscious 17-year-old, I didn't want to look uncool, or make a spectacle of myself. In the end, I wore my black dance leggings, a white cotton

T-shirt, and to finish off the ensemble, Mum's 1980s sweatband (I was certain I'd seen most runners wear those).

The real dilemma though was a bit more basic: how do you actually run outside? Obviously, I had run round a netball court, and on the athletics track, but doing it continuously on a pavement was completely different. I felt very clumsy as I plodded along the pavement and vigorously swung my arms back and forth. I was so embarrassed by my inability to look as if I was running effortlessly, and prayed I didn't pass anyone I knew. I deliberately kept my head down and aimed towards the park to avoid being seen or being hooted at by drivers.

God it was hard work! So much harder than I had anticipated. Within minutes I was huffing and puffing like an asthmatic pensioner. Good job I wore that retro sweatband! I got a stitch almost instantly which just made the run even more agonising. Tiny flies began buzzing in my face, one even got trapped in my eyelashes, and I nearly tripped over while trying to wipe it away. Running was turning out to be far more challenging and hazardous then I had ever imagined.

I did loads of sports weekly so considered myself fairly fit, but I was shocked at how much I struggled with continuous jogging. My mind was completely overtaken by the sheer effort of it all. I was determined not to stop because I knew it would be even harder to start again. In my head, I heard Dad say, 'Don't give up! you can do it!' which just about kept me going.

I estimated that I went for about 15–20 minutes before stumbling up my driveway and collapsing with exhaustion. My cotton T-shirt was drenched, and had gone transparent! I hadn't realised that until I got home, and I was mortified because I could see my bra underneath! My black dance leggings were plastered to my legs as well. I looked horrendous, and felt sick with cramp. Every muscle in my body was screaming with pain.

How come I wasn't a natural runner like Dad? He made it sound easy and blissful. He used to do this twice a day before

I was born! Why would he torture himself like this? What did he gain from it all?

I didn't get any sympathy from Mum and Natalie as I dragged myself back indoors. They told me that Dad had had a real talent for running; that maybe I should just give up on it now.

But I wanted to achieve something new. I still wanted to find something that would make it feel easier to think about Dad without getting upset. I wanted to follow his advice – and, quite literally, follow in his footsteps. But I felt like I had failed. After gulping several glasses of water and eventually peeling off my soaked clothes, I stood under the cool shower for a long time to wash away my misery. I just had to accept that I wasn't like Dad, I couldn't run like him, so I should just forget all about it.

But I couldn't.

What I didn't know that day was that I had caught the "runner's bug". Despite my disastrous first attempt at running, I couldn't let it go. I didn't want to completely admit defeat. The old saying "If at first you don't succeed try, try again" went round in my head for days afterwards. I had always been a competitive girl and never gave up because something was challenging.

I kept daydreaming of transforming myself into a professional sportswoman and making Dad proud. Every time I visited Dad's grave that summer it felt like I was letting him down. I knew he wouldn't give up so easily, so maybe I shouldn't either.

For the rest of the summer holidays, Natalie and I worked as many catering shifts as possible at a local hotel to earn some pocket money. It was tedious getting up at the crack of dawn to serve buffet breakfasts to greedy hotel guests but at least it gave me a focus and made the time go by faster.

It was such a relief to be back at college in September. Studying for my A2 exams suddenly became very intense as the workload increased. I was also aiming to do my driving exam in October so squeezed in as much practice as possible after college, and on weekends.

I was shaking with nerves as I sat in the driver's seat of my instructor's Mini Cooper at the test centre. So far, all of my friends had failed their driving exams, so I had the extra pressure of being the first to succeed.

My mind went blank as I fired up the engine. I panicked and instantly stalled the car as I attempted to pull away from the parking space. I mumbled an apology and tried again. I managed to jerkily get the car moving out of the centre and onto the main road. The rest of the test was a blur as I robotically followed the commands of the examiner. I was still shaking as I reversed the car back into the parking bay and turned off the engine at the end. My heart was thumping in my chest and I was holding back the tears, terrified of hearing the verdict.

I couldn't believe my ears as she congratulated me on passing. 'Pardon? I've passed?!' I was in disbelief, I couldn't move. My instructor came over, beaming. 'You've done it! Well done!' He had to help me out of the car and back into the passenger seat to drive me home, because I was still in shock. It wasn't until that evening when I told Mum the good news that it really sank in. Now I could be more independent. I was free to go where I wanted, when I wanted.

I knew that Natalie was happy for me too, but because of our rivalry, she struggled to show it. She took her exam the following day, and luckily she passed too. So that weekend we celebrated together. For the first time in ages, we were laughing together as we took it in turns driving each other around the town centre.

My favourite place to drive through was Windsor Great Park. I used to go there for picnics with my family when I was a little girl. Autumn was the best time to be there, when the trees were transforming themselves into stunning scarlet and bronze orbs. I loved that time of year. I liked walking in the woods near us, too, especially in the early evening when I could spot squirrels stuffing their cheeks with acorns and catch a glimpse of a couple of muntjac deer. Being among nature was revitalising.

I wanted to be out there more. I wanted to be free like the robins. So, this was the perfect time to try running again. I prepared myself properly by buying some running clothes and trainers. I also researched the right running technique so that I felt less spastic, and used my energy more efficiently. I didn't realise how much skill was involved, even in terms of not looking down, but forward, and landing on the mid-foot, not your heel.

I felt much more comfortable dressed in my new gear. I still got a stitch fairly early on in my run, but it felt less painful and eventually went once I got my breathing rhythm going. I concentrated on changing my running style. It felt strange at first, but after a while I got the hang of it. As I began to relax, I visualised running with Dad along the path. It made me smile and glow inside, and that really helped distract me from my aching limbs. My senses felt so alive. I noticed everything: the distinct bird tweets coming from the blackberry bushes, the hissing swans on the pond as I jogged round them, and the invigorating smell of oak trees carried on the breeze.

No one warned me about the dozens of cobwebs that flew in my face and hair though; I was constantly wiping them away. But that just made me feel more immersed in nature and I was transported into another world; one which was serene and beautiful.

I let my mind wander and kept on thinking about Dad, alive and well, running alongside me. I imagined chatting to him, and looking out for robins as we jogged by. I began to understand why people liked running. I liked the feeling of switching off from daily problems and leaving them all behind. My thoughts were consumed by my surroundings and my route. There wasn't any pressure to go very fast or far. I completely forgot about all my insignificant daily woes, and thought how happy Dad would be to see me following in his footsteps. I had escaped reality, I was with him, and we were free.

This small victory gave me my first experience of the "runner's high". It lasted the whole day, and I couldn't explain it any other way. My mind was buzzing, and I almost felt invincible now that I had overcome my running challenge. I felt a great weight had been lifted and I wanted to go again. I didn't want to lose this feeling. I felt stronger and so much more connected to Dad. Maybe I had inherited Dad's running talent after all?

One thing was for sure. That was the start of my new love / hate relationship with running.

CHAPTER 6

Going to University

I didn't want Christmas to arrive. Life's big events didn't feel right without Dad. And I was scared that it just wouldn't feel like Christmas without him.

Mum tried to get us into the spirit by carrying on with our usual festive rituals, but I didn't feel in the mood to rejoice. I felt guilty that Dad would be missing out.

Friends and family members invited us to spend Christmas day with them, but we declined all their invitations. We felt like we needed to get away from it all. Mum spontaneously suggested a skiing holiday over Christmas and new year to help take our minds off missing Dad. I hoped that waking up to a proper white Christmas would help bring back some of the magic of Christmas.

Dad had been a big fan of skiing. He used to go twice a season in his bachelor days and even persuaded Mum to go with him on several occasions before I was born. I'd been on a skiing trip at school, but we'd never been skiing as a family. Dad even told me that one of his greatest regrets was dealing with the realisation that he'd never be able to do any kind of sport ever again after the cancer had changed him. So Mum wanted to do this, in part, to fulfil Dad's wish for us to ski together.

St Anton in Austria was exactly how I imagined a traditional ski destination should be, with lots of snow, quaint shops to mooch around in, and plenty of hearty goulash dishes to tuck into. The change of scenery, clear air, and challenging slopes made me feel alive again.

I still missed Dad though, especially when we tried to tackle a black run for the first time. Dad would have zoomed down with ease showing us the shortest way to get to the bottom. But as inexperienced skiers, we ended up having to zig-zag downwards with our skis in "snowplough" position at snail's pace. It took ages but at least we reached the end without losing control and crashing.

I was jealous seeing all the other children with both parents, all having fun. I longed for my childhood years when we were a complete family celebrating together. But spending Christmas day in a different environment helped make the day less painful. I tried to forget all the usual family things we'd do at Christmas and embrace new ways of getting through the day. (And I was still glad to see a full stocking at the end of my bed when I woke up on Christmas day morning!)

2007 couldn't come around fast enough. I wanted a clean start; I was desperate to leave the horrors of 2006 behind.

Turning 18 in January was a big deal. It was the first birthday without Dad, and Mum went over the top to try to make it memorable for Natalie and me. Heaps of presents, balloons, personalised cakes ... and a special dinner with our closest friends at our favourite Italian restaurant. I couldn't stop smiling all day.

Mum kept us so busy, that it wasn't until we were back at home that I felt deflated and teary missing Dad. I wished he could have been there recording the day on his camcorder. I wanted to hear his voice and unwrap his latest hand-drawn card. That would have been the best birthday present.

It hadn't been a year since Dad had died. How long was that sense of loss going to last? Was I always going to feel like this? Could I ever be completely happy without him?

Later that evening, I asked Mum whether she still loved Dad; whether she could ever be entirely happy without him. She replied, 'Of course I do, no one can replace him. But Dad told me before he died that he wanted me to be happy, and to move on with my life. He doesn't want us to be mourning him forever. He loves us no matter what.'

Dad had given Mum his blessing to be free and to find new love, knowing that his death would separate them. I felt uplifted; it was wonderful to hear that Dad had loved and respected Mum so much that he wanted her to enjoy her life without him. And it was comforting to hear that he had given his blessing for us to carry on, and not worry about him. He had always been incredibly selfless, and I was so proud of him in that moment.

Mum told me something else that really helped me deal with all the conflicting feelings I'd been having. She said it was only natural that I would miss him, especially at family occasions, but that I shouldn't feel guilty about not thinking about him. Dad wouldn't have wanted that. He had only ever wanted us to be happy.

I tried to put myself in Dad's shoes and thought how heart-breaking it must have been for him when he was told he had cancer; knowing that he wouldn't live to see Natalie and me grow up. It must have been so horrible for him, knowing he was going to miss out on these special days, thinking about us experiencing them in his absence. And I realised then that I had to make the most of them – I had to stop feeling guilty and celebrate for him too.

March 4th marked one year since Dad passed away. I busied myself as much as possible to try to block out the flashbacks of him slowly slipping from our grasp. But it was impossible to hold back the tears. We visited his grave with flowers, and clung on to each for support. I couldn't believe we'd survived a whole year without him. I was surprised at how much we'd achieved.

When Dad died, I was worried about how we'd cope without him; in the past we'd relied on him for so much. Throughout the year it began to dawn on me that I had taken him for granted; I hadn't really appreciated all the little things he had done for me and my family. For example, without fail, Dad would polish all our footwear on a Sunday night, ready for the week ahead. It was easy to see how scruffy my boots and shoes were since he had died, because I hadn't been cleaning them like he used to.

It was the same with our garden. He was the only green-fingered person in our family and would tidy it up on Saturday afternoons. Since he'd died, we had completely neglected the garden and it had become meadow-like. In the end I took up the challenge of raking all the leaves and mowing the lawn which was back-breaking. I wished Dad was here to help, he had always made it look so easy, and he'd done it all without ever moaning.

He'd dealt with all the major things too: he'd looked after our insurance and finances, and kept everything ticking along smoothly. Mum now had the hard task of taking on all of those jobs, and I didn't like seeing her muddling her way through it all. I felt guilty that I couldn't help her, but I had no idea about that sort of thing.

Being a single parent now meant that Mum had to take responsibility for the whole household. At times, the pressure showed, and she snapped back if I offered to help. I shuffled away frustrated that I was so useless in those circumstances. It was unfair that Mum had to deal with all these things by herself. We didn't have any male relatives nearby to rely on and support us. Mum even said that she wished she "had a man around the house to help and lean on". Seeing her struggle made me anxious because I felt overwhelmed by all of her concerns, and I knew how hard it must have been, having no one to comfort her in the way that Dad could. I longed for him to stroll into the room and sort everything out.

Dad really had been our pillar of stability, and I'd never really appreciated that in the past. I felt like he had been our shepherd, guiding and protecting us. Without him, I felt vulnerable and lost. When he was at home with us it felt like our home was a safe, cosy haven. But after he was gone, there was less laughter in the house, particularly around meal times. I could sense Mum's tension. I could see how preoccupied she was with all the tasks she had to juggle, so we'd often sit in silence. I didn't want to irritate her even more, so thought it best to not say anything.

I didn't like being at home when it felt so awkward, because it just emphasised Dad's absence even more. Natalie and I would usually go upstairs to get out of Mum's way, and chat between ourselves. She'd often feel the same anxiety and annoyance that we couldn't help Mum. We were both still concerned about how we were going to get through everything. I was grateful to have someone who was able to understand exactly what I was going through, but there was no one for Mum to turn to. None of her friends or family members had been widowed, so she was alone in that respect.

The one reassurance I had was knowing what a fighter she was. She was strong willed enough to navigate her way through anything, and somehow she manged to keep us going, and keep us all afloat.

That was a huge step for me. That realisation that we were managing helped make our visits to Dad's grave feel a little bit different. As I stood there, huddled with Mum and Natalie, I felt more at ease and more content that we were getting by, and life was carrying on, and even going well.

I knew things could never go back to how they'd been when Dad was alive. Nothing and no one could replace him, so I stopped wishing things would go back to how they'd been. Dwelling on the past didn't help. It just made me more upset. I knew it was time to move forward and embrace the opportunities life was giving me. I knew deep down that Dad would want me to continue enjoying life and excelling in every way possible. So each day I forced myself to be positive, and to do my best for him.

With A level exams looming, my remaining time at college flew by. I was determined to get at least 3 A grades and secure my place at university. Mum had stepped into Dad's shoes, and chauffeured me around the country to view my top choice unis. I'd chosen to study Geography, and Exeter was my first choice. I hated revising in the summer months, I wanted to be outside in the sunshine, not stuck indoors with my head buried in books. My exams were spread out over two weeks, so I had plenty of time to prepare, and felt quietly confident that I had done enough to pass with good grades.

I barely slept the night before results day, and leapt out of bed to wait for the results to show up on the college website, way before 9.00am when they were due. I stared at the screen, poised on the edge of my stool refreshing the webpage every few seconds until they appeared ...

Three As! Yes! I'd been accepted into Exeter uni! Moments later, Natalie burst out of her room, just as jubilant, having been accepted by her first choice. We ran to find Mum and squealed our good news. We huddled and hugged, tears in our eyes. We'd done it! We were off to uni!

It still hadn't quite sunk in by September, but soon enough, I was packing up Mum's Toyota with everything apart from the kitchen sink. I'd never been away from home more than a week, and I was even more anxious because Natalie would be hundreds of miles away.

Over the summer, my love life had begun to blossom. I'd entered my first relationship with a guy, William, I'd met at a friend's 19th birthday party. He'd just finished his A levels too and was doing a gap year. He was well groomed, a rugby player, and very charming. I was instantly attracted to him. We hit it off straight away and went on a few dates before I set off for Exeter.

On the morning of me leaving for uni, he appeared on my doorstep with flowers to wish me bon voyage and promised to visit me within a week after I settled in. During those first few weeks, I was very homesick. Every day Mum texted to check I was okay and I'd respond with a reassuring message pretending I was fine. I didn't want to worry her, but I missed seeing Mum and Natalie every day.

At least my accommodation was homely and comfortable. I was lucky enough to be staying in a brand-new complex. It was like staying in a hotel. My bedroom had everything – en-suite and heated towel rail, double bed, mini fridge, kettle … there was even a kitchenette down the corridor if I didn't fancy eating in the canteen.

My boyfriend didn't let me down. After freshers' week he pulled up in his blue VW Polo and stayed with me in my catered halls for the weekend. It was so good to see him, and we spent our time shopping and trying out new eateries in the city. I felt much more at ease sharing my uni experience with someone I knew and cared about.

After he left on Sunday evening, I began to feel more confident and focused. The second week was when lectures began, and I was looking forward to meeting the people on my course.

I loved the Exeter campus because it was immersed in nature – so many trees, squirrels and seagulls! I did struggle with all the hills at first especially because my accommodation was at the bottom of "cardiac hill". Nine am lectures on a Monday were literally an uphill battle.

The city centre was only a mile away, so I walked there daily to browse around the shops and feel "normal." I didn't want to feel isolated in a student bubble. I even got a Saturday job to help pay for my train fares home.

Before long I was in the full swing of things as I joined several clubs, including fencing (I'd always wanted to release the swashbuckling Captain Jack Sparrow in me) and ballroom dancing (to coax out my Fred and Ginger talents). My boyfriend also visited one weekend a month, and I popped home on the train every 2–3 weeks to see Mum.

Christmas that year felt much easier. My boyfriend surprised me by arranging to stay at The Dorchester hotel in London just before Christmas. I'd never dreamt of staying in such a plush hotel and there I was, just 18 years old, mingling with the rich and famous. The only downside was the ridiculously miniscule portions at the Michelin star restaurant with eye-watering prices. I felt hungrier after the three-course meal than before it! But it was an experience I'll always treasure.

I hadn't been running much over the winter, just because I'd been so busy with my studies and trying out all sorts of other sports. But having lunch one Saturday at my boyfriend's house, his mum, Claire, suggested we went out for a run the next day. I knew Claire had run lots of marathons because all her finisher's photos were on display in their hallway, but I'd never considered talking about them before. I was intrigued because my dad had run the London Marathon, and now I'd experienced runner's high for myself.

Before long we got into a deep conversation about the wide world of running. I had no idea there were lots of local races happening almost every weekend, from 5k to ultramarathons. She told me she was running a 10k in a couple of months, and was eager to sign me and William up for it too. I was excited about it – especially when she said everyone got a medal for finishing, regardless of the time they crossed the finish line. That was motivation enough for me. And I knew it would be fun doing it with William, so I said, 'Yes, let's go for it!'

Through the winter, I committed myself to improving my running. I got a gym membership so I could practise 10k on a treadmill. God! It was mind-numbingly boring plodding on the machine for 45 minutes. But when I'd identified that it should take me just under an hour, I started practising outside – after all, the race would be on roads and contained hills, so I had to get used to the different conditions and the weather.

I was out every Sunday morning jogging along the River Exe which was far more interesting than the gym. Seeing other joggers, cyclists, and dog walkers helped make the time pass effortlessly, and fresh air was far more invigorating, compared with the stuffy gym.

The race day was cold and cloudy despite it being March. I was trembling with nerves as I walked with my boyfriend and his mum to the start line. The atmosphere was electric, with music being blasted from huge speakers, and a friendly group warm-up underway. I clung on to my boyfriend as we meandered to the start line.

Was I fit enough? Had I done enough training? Would I be slower than him?

What if I finished last?

I felt like an imposter as I lined up with all the professional-looking runners. There was no turning back though as I pinned my race number to my T-shirt.

I remembered Dad saying, 'Don't go off too quickly, pace yourself' as the runners quietened down waiting for the mayor to pull the trigger …

'On your marks, get set …' BANG!

We were off. Sort of. Because of the mass of people trying to get over the start line, we just shuffled at first. But then we began to spread out and find our pace. At first, I stuck with my boyfriend – who had set off rather fast – because I didn't want to get left behind. But by half way, his pace started to slow, and he was complaining of a stitch, so we agreed to separate. I carried on at a comfortable pace, feeling like a sheep, as I followed the other runners around the town.

I felt embarrassed at first, as hundreds of spectators waved and cheered as I passed. Kids called out my race number encouraging me on, and some even handed out jelly baby sweets. I didn't eat or drink the water offered en route, fearing I would spill it down me or choke.

Despite having covered the distance in practice, the race felt never-ending. I gasped with relief as I saw the "finish" banner flying. Only a few hundred metres to go.

'Come on, Gem! You can do it! Sprint as if Dad is waiting to meet you at the finish line!' I told myself.

My boyfriend had caught up by then and tried to grab my hand so that we could cross the finish line together, but I was determined to beat him. My competitive edge kicked in, and I sprinted ahead.

'Almost there, Gem! Final push! You can beat him!'

Whoosh! I flung myself over the red line sticking my chest out like the professionals do.

Cameras flashed and the crowd cheered. It felt as if everyone was looking at me.

I was tingling with the runner's high. There is no other feeling in the world to match it!

It was over, I'd done it!

A marshal approached me with a goodie bag. What a surprise! Inside were snacks like flapjacks and Mars bars, water, Lucozade and the most important thing: the medal. I felt like I'd won Gold at the Olympics. I proudly strung the medal around my neck and didn't take it off all day.

When my boyfriend joined me minutes later, he was furious that I hadn't slowed down to cross the line with him. He couldn't believe I'd beaten him. I guess I stole his thunder a bit, seeing as he was a rugby player, and supposed to be the faster one.

Did I care? Not really. For me the day wasn't about *us*. It was about *me*. I wanted my moment of glory. I'd wanted to do it for Dad. And I had done.

Now I was a proper runner.

For the rest of that year, I continued preparing for my next race. The more I ran, the more I missed it when I didn't run.

Going for a short jog always cleared my head and invigorated me. And the fact that it was free to do, anytime, anywhere, also made it appealing.

I passed all my Geography modules with flying colours, which was a huge relief. Now I could relax and enjoy a long summer break. And the main aim of my summer was to beat my 10k time at the Cancer Research Hampton Court race. This time I wasn't nervous. I was excited. I couldn't wait.

'Eyes on the prize,' I told myself as I set off on the big day. I went at my own pace this time without my boyfriend (whose pride was still dented). I was much more confident and enjoyed the stunning palatial gardens as I followed the route around.

It was a gorgeous summer's day, but the heat didn't affect me now that I'd invested in proper running shorts which kept me cool. I sailed through the finish line in a great time, and admired my new medal as I soaked up the atmosphere. I hadn't imagined there would be such camaraderie among the participants. Even though I was running with strangers, everyone was so smiley and encouraging.

I loved it.

The end of the summer holiday meant that I had to say goodbye to my boyfriend who was starting his own time at uni in York. He promised to be faithful to me, but I was beside myself with tears as I hugged him goodbye. It tore my heart knowing he'd be hundreds of miles away, having the time of his life without me.

Would I be able to trust him? What if he found another girl he fancied? Suppose he lost interest and didn't want to come home and visit me any more? I knew I had to block out those negative thoughts – and I'd had a lot of practice doing that – so I busied myself as much as possible to prove to myself (and him) that I was fine without him.

For my second and third years at uni, I lived with my three best male friends (they all had girlfriends so there was never any lovey-dovey awkwardness between us). We were on different courses, but hung out together as much as possible. One of the guys was my ballroom dancing partner, so we formed a special bond.

We rented a cheap, dilapidated terraced house a mile away from campus. There was just one mustard-coloured bathroom to share between us, so it was always a fight to get there first. But because the guys were all well mannered and respectful they usually let me have priority. They even stuck to the household chore I allocated them (hoovering, taking out the rubbish, etc.) except on a few Sunday mornings when I'd end up being "mother hen" clearing up after them after their heavy night of Xboxing and drinking.

My second year of study was more intense than the first, with more hours of lectures, long essays to write, and fieldtrips to go on. I also maintained a part-time job on campus to keep myself financially buoyant, but with my commitments to university societies, and my relationship with William in York, it all got a bit stressful at times.

Running became my escapism and was now an integral part of my routine; I always fitted in one or two hourly runs a week. I would feel worse if I didn't, and would rather get wet in the rain than be stuck indoors, feeling sorry for myself. I found the effort and concentration required for running, especially in bad weather, helped me to clear my head of all my worries, and gave me fresh perspective on things when it felt like life was getting too tough.

I set off on my runs from my student house, then did a loop around the campus and Exeter city centre. By the time I had run a few steps, I could already feel my head start to clear of all my worries. None of my friends ran, but they were always keen to find out when my next half-marathon was going to be, and how my training was going – and that encouraged me to keep it up and go on improving my race times.

Now that William was at York, we didn't see each other as much, and that began to take its toll on me emotionally. We still spoke every day, but I'd be secretly jealous when I'd hear he'd been having a whale of a time without me. I wanted to be a bigger part of his life. Sometimes he was too busy to call which made me so angry. How could he not find time to speak to his girlfriend?!

Was I overreacting? Maybe I was just being paranoid and feeling insecure because of the distance? I'm sure he must have had some of the same feelings when I'd left for Exeter. How on earth had he managed?

I didn't want to be an annoying, clingy girlfriend so any time I felt overwhelmed, or "discarded" by him, I'd get changed into my running gear and go outside to vent my feelings. Running fast in the fresh air gave me the space to release my emotions without screaming and crying. I was able to expel all my negative feelings and return home feeling calmer and better about myself. The adrenaline rush was my antidote. Regardless of how rubbish I felt before heading out, I always got home feeling happier.

Running became an even more regular part of my routine leading up to Christmas; and I could always justify it knowing that it was helping me physically and emotionally. I looked forward to my runs and made sure I kept fitting them into my schedule because I wanted to keep on building up my stamina. For the first time ever on Christmas day, I got up early – not to unwrap the presents in my stocking, but to do a short jog before Natalie and Mum got up. I knew it would lift my spirits and set me up for the day, so I crept out of bed and got changed into my running gear. I tip-toed downstairs and out quietly.

It was bizarre running in the semi-light. The roads were completely deserted. I felt bleary-eyed and stiff at first, my limbs not wanting to co-operate as I forced them into motion. But after a few minutes of slow plodding, I began to wake up and warm up.

I passed houses twinkling with fairy lights and shining with a friendly glow. Some families were already up opening their presents, and soon the air would be dense with the familiar smell of roast turkey. I waved at walkers with dogs wearing tinsel and antlers.

I could only manage 30–40 minutes before my tummy began to rumble so I returned home for breakfast feeling energised and excited about the day. To my relief Mum and Natalie were still fast asleep. I hadn't woken them, and they were completely oblivious to the fact I'd already been out when they finally emerged from their beds.

That Christmas was a joyful time for the three of us. For the first time since losing Dad, we resumed our family festive traditions: real tree, too many decorations, stockings … I felt like I had been looking forward to Christmas for the first time in years. I assumed Dad's old role of filming and photographing the day for posterity. I really wanted Mum to relax that Christmas, so I offered to cook. I had never done a roast before, but I relished cooking in my student house, so embraced the challenge of doing a turkey with all the trimmings. My homemade Yorkshire puddings puffed up perfectly, and I managed not to burn anything.

I felt as if I had grown accustomed to just three of us sitting around the table. Meal times weren't awkward or difficult as they had been in the first few weeks or months after we'd lost Dad. Natalie and I chatted away non-stop about our different lives at uni, and we had Christmas tunes playing in the background. It was cosy and fun celebrating together; it was everything I'd hoped it would be.

Dad used to buy the best presents for us to give to Mum, so I hadn't ever had to worry about what to get her. Now though, it was up to me and Natalie to come up with something special for her each year. And we really wanted to spoil her because she had done so much to keep our family going. She wasn't into the usual chocolates and bubble bath, so I had to rack my brains to think of something unique.

After chatting to Natalie, we decided to buy tickets for the *Cinderella* ballet at the Royal Opera House in London, with the money I'd saved from my uni job. We'd all loved dressing up and going to the theatre every year with Dad, so it felt like it was high-time that we went again. I was delighted when she unwrapped the tickets and was grinning from ear to ear. We were all very excited and couldn't wait to see the performance in a few months' time.

In the afternoon we visited Dad's grave to lay a wreath. We always wanted to feel like we were still including him. But I tried not to feel too sad as I wished him a Happy Christmas. I knew he wouldn't want me to be upset, so I did my best to remain cheerful and upbeat for his sake. I hoped that Dad was watching us from above, and that his spirit was present in the robins around us.

I dreaded the end of the winter break because it meant I'd be separated from my boyfriend again. I had to distract myself as much as possible down in Exeter to stop my mind wondering what he was up to in York.

But there was always running to focus on. Determined to stay on track with it, I entered myself for a half-marathon in my hometown, in May. Now that I had booked my place, there was no excuse, no turning back. I had to be committed to the training.

I splashed out on a new pair of Nike endurance trainers and a professional Garmin sports watch which included GPS so that I couldn't get lost! My boyfriend's mum also gave me all her *Runner's World* magazines for "bed time reading" to help me prepare. I was beginning to feel like a serious runner. It wasn't just a hobby, it was becoming a lifestyle.

The race day seemed to arrive quickly. I'd only run up to 12 miles in training, so I prayed that I had enough energy to reach the finish. It was an 8.30am start, but I was wide awake before 6.00am. My boyfriend surprised me by turning up, just as I was lining up to start. I was so thrilled to see him, and so touched that he came from York to support me. With him waiting at the end, I knew I had to complete it, I couldn't let him down.

'Steady and consistent like the tortoise, don't sprint like the hare,' I thought to myself. 'Pace yourself – don't go too fast and burn out!'

The route was quite easy to begin with. There were no major hills to climb, and because I knew the area well I didn't get too distracted by the sights. I just focused on my watch and keeping to the pace I'd set myself.

But at miles 7–8 there was a killer incline that seemed never-ending. All I could see were the hunched runners in front of me, pumping their arms furiously as they made their way upwards. I was beginning to fade until a runner dressed as a dinosaur overtook me!

'What? A dinosaur! I can't let a dinosaur beat me. Right, Gem, come on! Dad would be laughing if he saw you now, you have to speed up!' I gritted my teeth, began to accelerate, and caught up with the Womble, waving as I ran past.

From the ninth mile, I set myself a new goal. 'Okay, Gem, let's play a game. How many runners can I overtake? Pick a target and aim for them!' The more people I beat, the better.

I constantly checked my watch to make sure I kept to my race time target. I knew I just had to keep on going and not slow down.

With the final mile in sight, the crowds of spectators began to thicken, and I could hear the live DJ calling out race numbers as they crossed the line. As I re-entered the grounds of the stately home where the race started and finished, I heard my boyfriend yell, 'Go, Gem! Nearly there! Final push!'

It was my moment of glory. 'Smile, Gem,' I told myself. 'Try not to look hideous for the cameras!' Moments later I crossed the finish line, hearing the electronic bleep recording my time.

I slowed down to a jog and then a walk, trying to catch my breath. I was speechless.

I'd actually completed a half-marathon race!

I was trembling as I received my big red medal, and gulped down a whole bottle of water.

My boyfriend strode towards me smiling and congratulating me as we embraced. I was in disbelief for hours afterwards. I clutched my medal as if it was my most precious possession, like Gollum from *Lord of the Rings*.

I wanted to run again. It felt like there was so much energy coursing through my body. I wanted to do another race and see if I could run even faster – and get another medal for my collection. How I wished that Dad could have seen it. I imagined that if he'd been alive, he'd have run with me – how amazing it would have felt to cross the finish line together.

Now I knew I had to go on running. I wanted to make Dad proud.

The next morning, I grabbed my laptop and searched for half-marathons in my area in the summer / autumn. Windsor half-marathon in September was the nearest, so without hesitation, I secured my place. Now I had the whole summer to improve my running and look forward to another race.

Throughout the summer I began running more frequently, and for longer. Without fail, I was out every Saturday and Sunday morning plus once or twice during the week, regardless of the weather (yes, it does rain frequently in British summertime!).

I devised different routes around the woods, which were hilly, but far more interesting than running on pavements. I liked the solitude and enjoyed immersing myself in nature. Whenever I felt tired and my body begged me to give up, I would picture Dad alongside me, encouraging me. I googled positive mantras which I memorised and told myself over and over again to try to boost my resolve.

'Temporary pain for eternal glory.'

'Eyes on the prize!'

And the classic: 'No pain, no gain!'

Everything was building towards Windsor race day. My excitement was building, but I was frustrated by the start time: 1.00pm! Why start a running race in the middle of the day?! I was eager to get going, but had to try to keep calm and save my energy.

I'd never done a race beginning so late in the day, so I was worried that I'd get hungry and run out of steam if I didn't eat something before the start. (As the start neared, my 7.00am porridge was starting to feel like a very long time ago.) I knew it would be impossible to run on a full stomach, so I took a leaf out of my dad's book and opted for peanut butter on wholemeal toast (no banana) at 11.30am. Huge mistake!

My boyfriend's mum joined me for the race, while William himself lazed in the sun, waiting for us to finish. It was boiling at 1.00pm. Twenty-five degrees and no breeze. The route consisted of two laps around Windsor Great Park. By the fifth mile, I was already tired and bored by the scenery. It was depressing thinking I'd have to do another lap along the same uneven, pebbly path.

But the more pressing issue was my stomach. Having not left enough time before eating and running I had "runner's trot" for the first time, and had to make an emergency pit stop in a portacabin toilet.

I was fuming! I'd never stopped mid-run before and felt physically ill because of the peanut butter toast. The blazing sun and humidity was also getting to me. I knew that I'd really messed up my chances of getting a better half-marathon time, and I hated it.

I refused to give up though, and forced myself to carry on after the pit stop. Dad wouldn't have thrown in the towel, and neither would I. Finally, the finish line came into sight. I tried to sprint towards it, but my stomach pains were so bad I just couldn't. I completed the race eight minutes slower than my first half-marathon which really dampened the day for me. Even the medal, which was a stunning, huge gold disk, engraved with Windsor castle, couldn't cheer me up.

I couldn't believe how silly I'd been to mess up my eating pattern. Why hadn't I practised running in the afternoon? My body simply hadn't liked it, and rebelled. I certainly paid the price.

My boyfriend did his best to lift my spirits, but I wasn't in the mood. I was too impatient and sweaty. I just wanted to go home and shower.

It was a real learning curve for me. I realised there were good and bad races. I knew it couldn't always go smoothly, and that there would always be things that were out of my control, like the weather and race time. I had to adapt. I had to put it behind me and move on.

Fuelled by anger from my disappointing Windsor experience, I began planning the next year's races. I was determined to do at least three different races every year and increase my medal hoard. Running was no longer a leisurely pastime; it had become a very competitive sport.

CHAPTER 7

Running with Heartache

I tried to forget about my poor running performance at the Windsor half-marathon, but I couldn't let it go. I was still furious with myself a week later when I left home to return to Exeter. I didn't want to go back for my final year because I knew it was going to be stressful, and I didn't know how I was going to handle that pressure. It had all come around so quickly, I thought the three years would drag out, but the time had flown. I was worried that if I didn't get at least a 2:1 grade at the end, it would harm my employment chances, and, if I couldn't get a decent job, then all my years of education, costing literally thousands of pounds, would have been a waste!

I couldn't fall at the final hurdle ... I had to make Mum and Dad proud and prove that it had all been worth it.

My overall degree grade depended on the summer exams and 10,000-word dissertation. I was used to writing 2,000–3,000-word essays but not 10,000! To get ahead, I'd done all my research and reading during the summer, so in theory, all I had to do was condense my notes and produce a convincing, coherent piece of writing. Easier said than done! How on earth was I going to start this marathon-long essay?

Overwhelmed with my studies I found myself more homesick than ever. I really missed seeing my boyfriend. Despite speaking most nights, the long periods of not being in his arms made my heart ache. The constant wind and rain in the south-west of England depressed me too; it felt like I was enduring day after day of walking to and from campus, getting drenched.

I was craving home, and comfort, and Mum's special fried rice. I counted down the days (literally ticking them off on my desk calendar) until my next trip home.

Without fail, Mum would be at the station on the Friday evening, waiting for me. I'd run all the way along the platform, up the escalators, and into the foyer with my mini suitcase twisting and turning behind me. I didn't stop until I reached Mum's embrace. Coming home was the best feeling in the world. It's what spurred me on during my weeks at uni. I worked hard knowing that I could look forward to relaxing with Mum at home and getting a good night's sleep in my comfy bed.

Mum knew I needed to feel that I could come home whenever I needed to, so she let me take the Fiat Punto she had bought Natalie when we were learning to drive. Two of the guys I lived with also had Fiat Puntos, so we had a blue "Fiat Fleet" parked outside our house.

Mum also pulled out all the stops to make sure that Natalie and I celebrated our 21st birthday in style. She booked a private dining room at The Berkeley hotel (which was run by Gordon Ramsay at the time). We had a bespoke three-course menu with canapes and champagne. Mum even splashed out on two custom-made, multi-tiered cakes, which Natalie and I designed.

I spent ages choosing a suitable dress for lunch; nothing too glamorous and glitzy because it was a daytime event, but something eye-catching and pretty. I missed Dad being there to help me decide, like he had at our prom. He was always good at knowing what to wear. I found *the dress* eventually which was pink and black, while Natalie opted for a deep blue one (usually I'd be in blue and Natalie in pink so that made a fun change).

Snow was forecast on the day of our birthday, but that didn't stop me nipping out for a quick run at the crack of dawn. It was freezing outside, but I stayed warm under the layers of thermals I'd piled on. I returned invigorated and bubbling with excitement for our big day up in London.

When we got to The Berkeley, my boyfriend was already there, looking handsome in his suit, and he helped us decorate the room we'd booked. Our elaborate cakes were the centrepiece, and everyone admired them as they walked in.

The food was exquisite, and the staff surprised Natalie and me with a special dessert, each with our names written in chocolate. With our huge cakes lit with lots of candles, and everyone singing 'Happy Birthday', I felt a wave of emotion wash over me as I reflected on my life, and my thoughts reached out to Dad. I couldn't help think if only he'd been standing opposite me with his camcorder, singing and shouting 'Make a wish!' like he used to ...

I blinked away the tears in my eyes and pulled myself together. It was a day for celebrating, and I refused to be sad – Dad wouldn't have wanted me to be upset. I had all my close family and friends around me, and reminded myself of the words on Dad's gravestone: "Gone from home but not from our hearts". Dad may not have been there physically, but he was definitely in my heart, and would always be a part of any celebration.

I'm not good at public speeches, and I was just too emotional to say anything, so Mum stepped in to say a few words to our supportive friends and family. I kept my head down and concentrated on cutting my cake.

It was late by the time we reached home, the car bursting with gifts. I wished I didn't have to go back to uni. I wanted to stay at home and not have to face the thought of that dissertation, or the looming exams.

Back in Exeter, I spent every spare moment furiously typing to get the dissertation done. I very nearly threw my printer out the window when it decided to pack up in the middle of printing it. After breaking down in tears, one of my housemates stepped in to help me. We used his printer, and we finally managed to get it all done, late in the evening the night before I had to hand it in. The immense feeling of self-satisfaction was worth all the pain, and after I'd given it in, I practically skipped down the road with glee.

That Easter I ran in the same 10k race for the third year in a row, and was eager to get my fastest time yet. I was far more confident now that I had a set routine. I had precise timings of when to get up, eat, and drive to the venue. My boyfriend reluctantly joined in again, but had resigned himself to the fact that he was never going to beat me. I knew the course like the back of my hand which helped with my pacing, so I could cover more ground more quickly on flatter parts, and save energy for the inclines. I knocked off two minutes from the previous year's race, so was very chuffed as I waited for my boyfriend and his mum to finish.

Fizzing with joy that I had redeemed myself from the disastrous Windsor half-marathon, I booked two more races that year – another 10k in the summer, and a half-marathon in the autumn. Entering these races was beginning to add up though. On average a 10k was £20 and a half-marathon £30. I didn't mind though if the money was going towards a charity – as long I got a medal and goodie bag at the end!

I soon came back down to earth from my runner's high after the Easter break and returned for the final term of summer exams. Late one evening in May, I was sprawled out on my bed, among a sea of paper and highlighters, cramming in revision notes, when my boyfriend rang for our usual evening chat. He sounded quieter than usual and more serious.

'Gem, I can't come home this weekend to see you, I've got too much going on at uni. I'm really struggling to find time for this relationship and making it work. I'm really sorry but I don't think I can do this any more.'

I couldn't understand him. I was in the same boat; I hated being so far apart and making the long journeys to see each other, but I still looked forward to seeing him. I said, 'I want to make this work – why can't you? Don't you love me any more …?'

There was a long pause.

'No, it's not that. It's just … well, other girls have been taking an interest in me. Don't worry, I've not kissed them or anything, but a part of me thinks it would be so much easier if I was single and could date someone up here.' He said it was too expensive and too stressful coming back to see me, but I couldn't really focus on what he was saying any more. We went round in circles for half an hour, as I got more and more upset and angry. Why was he saying all of this now, when I was in the midst of revising for finals? Why was he being so inconsiderate?!

Finally, I persuaded him to come home that weekend, so that we could discuss it face-to-face when we weren't both so tired. My heart sank I as put my phone down. I couldn't concentrate on Geography, my mind was racing with questions: had he cheated on me and was trying to cover it up? Were we really going to break up? What would I do without him?

I didn't sleep at all, his words echoed in my head, and I couldn't stop myself imagining him having fun with other girls in York. I felt like I couldn't lose him, I had to win him back!

He drove over to my house the following Saturday afternoon. I tried to be chirpy, but he was so cold and withdrawn; he couldn't even look me in the eye.

We sat on the sofa and I waited for him to explain himself before I erupted.

'We've been together three years! You can't just throw that all away because "it's too difficult"! If you truly loved me, distance wouldn't be an issue. I know it's a long way, but I manage because I want to be with you. Why have you changed?'

He kept repeating himself, simply saying he couldn't commit to a long-distance relationship any more. This was his last trip home. The sole reason he came was to break up with me and there was nothing I could do.

I was stunned into silence, and I couldn't hold back the tears any longer.

He said this was the hardest decision for him to make, but it was the right one. He wanted to stay friends, but thought it best if we didn't speak for a while so we could give each other the breathing space we needed to move on. He tried to hug me goodbye, but I refused. I stood at the front door in a daze as I watched him drive away. I hoped he would do a U-turn and come back, saying he'd made a mistake, that he wanted to try to make our relationship work.

But he didn't. He was gone.

I was in hysterics for the rest of the day. Mum found me in a heap on the sofa, clutching a box of tissues. She tried to comfort me, and held me tightly, saying he didn't deserve me and that I could do better. I didn't want someone else though, I wanted him.

I thought running might help, but I had no energy.

How was I going to survive being by myself again? I was so used to talking to him every night before bed, how was I going to sleep now without hearing his voice?

I felt sick and dehydrated. I lost my appetite. Mum tried to coax me to eat her chicken and courgette risotto which I usually devoured, but I barely touched it. I didn't know what to do with myself. I was in limbo again.

It wasn't as if my boyfriend had died and I would never see him again. It wasn't like Dad. This was different; I knew he was still there – he just didn't want to be with me any more. I'd been rejected for the first time in my life.

Why wasn't I good enough?

Had he been sleeping with other girls?

How long had he felt like this?

I didn't deserve this. I'd spent three years of my life devoted to him. Had it all been a waste?

How was I going to get over him? Nothing I did could distract me from thinking of him. I kept looking at the photos of us together on Facebook and re-reading his old texts. I didn't want to delete him from my life. He had been my first true love. I couldn't just forget him.

I didn't sleep that night hoping that he might call or text. But he didn't.

Was I really single again?

I delayed my return to Exeter. I couldn't face my friends and tell them what had happened. Mum was very supportive and took time off work to be with me. She kept me occupied with errands, and helping her to sort out Grandad's old house after he'd moved into a care home nearby.

The house had been Mum's childhood home; she had lived there from the age of eight, when the family had moved from Hong Kong. My mum, uncle, grandma and grandad had emigrated to make a better life for themselves. Sifting through Mum's things in her old bedroom helped me shift my emotions and stopped me feeling so sorry for myself.

It was comforting being back in my grandad's house – it hadn't changed since he bought it over 40 years ago. The décor was still a 1970's brown / orange with dark green carpet in the hallway. The rooms smelt of mothballs (my grandad had them stored in all the wardrobes and his suit-pockets) and there was still a pile of pears and apples by the back door from his little orchard, just as I remembered there always had been.

It had been a huge upheaval moving Grandad to a nursing home near us, but he was too elderly and too ill to live alone.

Mum was tearful the day she handed the keys over to the new owners, but it meant she could stop worrying about Grandad living by himself. It was a sad time for them as it was the closing of a significant chapter of their lives, but ultimately the right decision.

As June arrived, I knew I couldn't just mope about any longer. At the back of my mind I knew had to get back into revision mode. I couldn't waste all the effort I'd put into my degree now, just because I'd broken up with my boyfriend. I wanted to prove I was stronger and better without him. I de-friended him on Facebook, I didn't want to be tempted to see what he was doing in York.

I blasted Destiny's Child songs 'Survivor' and 'Independent Woman' in my headphones as I sat on the train back to Exeter. I could do this! I didn't need him to succeed and be happy!

My exams were over within a week, and I didn't hang around much afterwards. I packed everything up from my rented house and said goodbye to my housemates. It was emotional leaving my second home, and all my friends behind. Like Mum, I was closing a chapter too.

When I found out that I'd achieved my aim of a 2:1, the rest of the summer felt much more carefree. I organised some work experience in a Planning Consultancy to see if it could be a potential career path. The office had a relaxed vibe. I liked working with the landscape designers and using my geography knowledge and creative skills. Perhaps this was the way forward for me?

I spent a lot of time with Natalie that summer. We wore new dresses and fascinators to Royal Ascot; I'd always wanted to go since the days when we used to see all the outrageous outfits as Dad drove us home from school. I enjoyed pulling up in my little car, and parking alongside all the Bentleys and Ferraris. I even saw the Queen quite close up as she was handing out an award in the parade ring.

We went to see *Swan Lake* at the Royal Albert Hall too. I'd booked tickets to go with my ex- boyfriend months ago, but it was even more fun going with Natalie. I was almost in tears as I felt Odette's pain at seeing her lover being tricked and betraying her. Thank goodness there is a happy ending as she is saved by her prince.

My second running race of the year – another 10k – followed in July. Natalie offered to come and support me which I was thrilled about. It meant I had a little extra pressure to run even faster, and I set a new personal best time. I managed shave off 2 minutes, despite the boiling sun, so I was delighted. I booked my next race – London's *Run to the Beat* half-marathon in September, as soon as I got home. And this time I wasn't going to mess it up, whatever time of day it started!

I had to make one more trip to Exeter first though – for my graduation in August. Natalie and I went down the night before – for one last shopping spree and a bit of a celebration, and Mum joined us for the big day.

I leapt out of bed at 6.00am to do my last three-mile run round the city before breakfast. It was a bright and breezy day, and I felt calmer as I stretched and admired the stunning views from the campus. I was really going to miss living in Exeter. I wouldn't miss the noisy seagulls waking me up each morning of course, but I certainly was going to miss the freedom and the independence I'd had.

I felt very grown up as I put on my new white blouse and black skirt underneath the heavy robes and mortar board. I couldn't believe I was graduating, it felt like I was in my own personal chick-flick. Neither Mum nor Dad had been to university, so this was a very special and significant day for my family.

The awards ceremony took place in the large, historic theatre, and I was shaking with nerves as my name was read out and I walked across the stage in my high heels. The Vice Chancellor gave me a firm hand shake as she handed me my certificates, but

I didn't hear what she said, so just smiled and concentrated on not falling down the steps to get off the stage.

I saw Mum and Natalie in the audience waving at me, but I didn't want to embarrass myself by waving back. I thought of Dad, and imagined he would be cheering and whistling loudly if he were sitting there too, no doubt recording it all on his camcorder. I wished he was there, I hoped he would have been proud of what I'd accomplished.

Once the official photo of Geography graduates 2010 was taken outside, with all of us throwing our mortar boards in the air, I said goodbye to my friends and went for lunch in the city with Mum and Natalie. I was still proudly dressed in my gown, and making the most of it! But it was rather cumbersome; the wind kept billowing it up like a sail, and trying to eat with it on wasn't easy, but I was just enjoying my moment.

On the journey home, a huge sense of relief washed over me. It was all over. My university life was complete.

Natalie's graduation was a few days later in Warwick and we repeated the same process. We both attained 2:1 degrees so there was no bickering about who did better.

After the excitement, I couldn't help feeling a little lost without a clear career direction. A Geography degree is very versatile, but I didn't want to be a Geography teacher or study rivers (the usual paths people follow). Town Planning seemed like the logical choice, having already done work experience in that area and knowing I liked it. I needed a Master's degree first though, so I enrolled on a full-time one-year Development Planning Master's degree at Reading university, starting that October.

But first, the half-marathon …

By now, Mum was on-board with my running passion and wanted to come and watch me. Having Mum's support was really important to me. Mum or Dad had always been there to cheer me on in my sporting ventures when I was younger, and

I'd really hoped she'd be there to watch me this time. I was so happy when she volunteered to drive me and make a big day out of it in London. Being able to share my triumphs (and my disappointments) with her made running more meaningful. And spending the time together (even if it was at 7.00am on a wet Sunday morning journey to the O2 Arena in Greenwich) felt like a mini-adventure. It felt like it brought us closer together too.

I was feeling restless and wanted to get going before I got too hungry. I didn't want any tummy problems like at the Windsor half-marathon! But the race was delayed because of roadworks, and by the time we were summoned into our starting pens, at 11.15, it felt like a very long time since breakfast.

This was the largest race I'd ever participated in. Thousands of runners of all ages and nationalities lined up wearing foil capes to keep the rain off. As there were so many taking part, the race organisers had to start the runners off in heats depending on their predicted finish time – the faster times went first. I waved goodbye to Mum and found my "sub-1hour 45min" section near the front, so luckily so I didn't have long to wait to get going.

The race was flat and fast, despite the wet conditions. Each mile had a live band playing music hence the name Run to the Beat – and it gave me a lift as I passed. I particularly liked the Caribbean drummers – very summery and uplifting! The route wasn't particularly interesting, but the hordes of crowds cheering on the pavements kept me motivated.

By mile 12 I knew I could achieve another personal best time, and the thought of seeing Mum at the end helped energise me. I was coasting to the finish – 1 hour and 41 minutes! Yes! So much better than the Windsor half-marathon. I was jumping up and down, absolutely elated as I clutched my new medal and tried to find Mum.

It was very chaotic in the car park, and I couldn't find her. I didn't have my phone with me, so I had to borrow a marshal's mobile to call her. Half an hour later we found each other. I was very upset that she'd missed me crossing the line. I'd run my best race yet and she hadn't seen it. Mum was equally disappointed. She'd been having a coffee in the O2 to stay warm; she hadn't realised just how fast I was going to be!

We drove to central London for a Chinese Dim sum. We used to go as a family several times a year, but that was one of those traditions that had faded away after Dad died. Chinatown was adorned in red and gold lanterns and lights for the Chinese Moon Festival, and there was a lively atmosphere, as Chinese families and tourists took in the sights.

As soon as my steamed dumplings and char sui pork arrived, I relaxed, and really began to enjoy spending time with Mum. Other diners stared at me, sitting there in my T-shirt and shorts, but I didn't care. I was happy chatting to Mum, and proud to be showing off my medal. By the time I got home though, I couldn't wait to get out of my running gear and have a hot shower. My muscles ached because I'd pushed myself so hard in the race … but it had really paid off.

My Master's course began the following week, and I was feeling the anxiety. It felt like a huge step up from my BA degree. What if everyone was brighter than me? Supposing I looked stupid in front of them? How much studying and preparation had they done? Had I even made the right decision enrolling on the course?

As I followed the dozens of international and mature students into the lecture room, I realised I was one of the youngest, and felt a little out of place. I perched myself at the end of the row near the exit so that I could slip out if I found it too overwhelming. The course modules included subjects I'd never covered before like Economics, which I'd been dreading. The last time I'd done proper Maths was at GCSE level, and back then, I'd been pretty pleased with my B grade.

Already I was beginning to feel stressed, and this was just day one! Maybe I had made a huge mistake?

CHAPTER 8

The London Marathon

I couldn't wait to get away after my first day of lectures. I really felt like I was swimming against the tide and this was only the beginning. I didn't want to go back the next day. I wanted to run away, and give up on my ambition of completing a Master's degree.

I didn't like feeling like I was the bottom of the class. I didn't want to risk failing or just scraping a pass. I felt as if everyone expected me to do well because I always had done, but this stretched way beyond my comfort zone.

I hit the gym on my way home to try to release some of the tension. Since the summer I'd adopted a new exercise routine. I'd read that it was beneficial for runners to do resistance training and use the bike and cross trainer in the gym on non-running days to strengthen the body. So I had started running 3–4 days a week, and cross-training at the gym on the other days.

I was exercising almost every day now. But I found that it really helped me mentally and physically, to feel focused and motivated.

I was grouchy on the rare occasions I didn't do anything. I'd feel lazy and lethargic, and I hated that more than anything. Maintaining and improving my fitness became more and more of a priority, because it made me feel so good.

I *did* go back to uni.

There were only two full days of lectures on Monday and Tuesday, which meant I'd go to the gym on the way home. On the other days I could study at home and go for a run whenever I liked – in theory. But really, because the modules were so much more challenging than I'd anticipated, and required so much group work and site visits, they were completely crammed with work.

We also had to do quite a few presentations in front of all the students and the professors, which I hated. It wasn't just that I hated public speaking; I didn't really understand it. I'd always rush through my notes and talk so quickly for fear of boring the listeners. No matter how many times I rehearsed a presentation I'd still feel underprepared and have sleepless nights.

Going for a jog, or pedalling endlessly on a bike at the gym seemed like the best ways for me to cope with the anxiety, and bolster my self-confidence. When I run or cycle, my breathing is controlled, and my mind is solely focused on my surroundings and on where I'm going. No distractions, just me and nature.

I also had to do a 10,000 word "Independent Project". I particularly enjoyed the idea of redesigning an urban or rural area to make it more efficient and attractive for people. My own town was being redeveloped at the time, and I got completely absorbed in taking photos, conducting surveys and meeting retail owners. I felt more connected to my local environment and it made me realise I could see myself actively working in this industry once I completed my degree.

The autumn term trickled by, and I started to find my feet. It helped that I made some new friends who were just as mind boggled as me with some of our modules.

I was always looking ahead to my next race.

My first race of 2011 was the Maidenhead Easter 10 Mile on Good Friday. It was very hot, already over 20 degrees when we set off at 10.00am, but with Mum waiting at the finish line, I had all the inspiration I needed to spur me on.

'Keep going, Mum's waiting – make her and Dad proud,' I kept telling myself.

As soon as the finish banner was in sight, I sprinted for it. I spotted her and waved, which gave me an extra boost of energy, and helped me overcome the awful stitch I'd been carrying. It wasn't the fastest 10 miles I'd run but not too bad. I was just relieved to get it over with, and so pleased that Mum had seen me run. She was immensely proud and took lots of photos. I was still glowing with pink cheeks the rest of the day and hung my new medal with the others on my bedroom wall. One race down, two to go.

I booked my place for the inaugural Maidenhead half-marathon in September, and that left me enough time to train for another race in the summer. I chose to do the same 10k I'd done with my ex-boyfriend. I'd done the race for three consecutive years and wanted to prove to myself that I could do it without him. And, of course, I wanted to push myself to try to achieve a new PB.

It was strange driving to the venue on the morning and not meeting up with him and his mum before the race started. I hadn't spoken to him since we'd broken up. I still had mixed feelings about him. Half of me wanted to spot him and hug him like we used to, but then the other half of me resented him for the break-up and didn't want to see him ever again.

Even though it had nearly been a whole year since we broke up I was still scarred by the heartbreak and often wondered what life would have been like if we'd stayed together.

Suppose he was at the race? What if he was running with a new girlfriend?

I realised then that I didn't want to know. Ignorance is bliss, I told myself.

The race went well, and I soared round, fuelled by all of that lingering pain and anger. I got a new PB, and several other runners were impressed by my performance. They assumed I ran for a club or was a semi-professional. I'd never considered joining a club and was flattered by their compliments.

Maybe I should join a club? Could I make a career out of running?

Curious, I had a taster session with my local running club. The other runners were mainly mature men and women; I was the youngest by far. They met several evenings a week for an hour's run around the woods, or along roads in the winter. I'd never run in the evening because I was always too tired by then; I preferred getting it done in the morning, so it didn't feel like it was hanging over me all day. I found running with others frustrating too; I didn't feel I could just run at my own pace because I felt compelled to chat on the go, and that just gave me a stitch.

I decided that a running club wasn't for me and carried on training by myself. Running was "me time" – time to clear my thoughts and take complete control over my speed and distance, which is what I wanted.

I realised how much running meant to me when I went on our week-long fieldtrip to France and Germany in the second term. I wasn't able to go for my usual runs and I missed them so much. I was dying to put my trainers on and run for even just 30 minutes outside, but I didn't get the chance with our jam-packed schedule. At least we did lots of walking around various cities, but I was so relieved to be on the Eurostar home, knowing I could go for a run the next morning.

My exams were fairly early in May and I was feeling the pressure. On the morning of my Economics exam I didn't even go on the run I had planned because I was feeling so paranoid I hadn't done enough revision. I ended up spending every last minute cramming in as much information as possible. I was memorising complex formulae and practising numerous calculations right up until we went into the examination hall. The exams were as hard as I'd feared, and I ran out of time to double check my answers. I was panicking. How could I not have time to go over my answers?!

I was furious with myself as I put down the pen; I should have written faster so that I had enough time to go over everything. I wondered if anyone else had struggled with the exam too, but I wasn't in the mood to talk about it. The thought of comparing my answers with others made me feel even worse so I just drove home.

I was relieved that it was over. I was exhausted mentally, but fired up physically. So, as soon as I got back, I went for a run. I had to do something to channel all that anxiety and adrenaline. Being back in the woods was the best antidote. I sprinted up and down the hills, soaking up the warm sunshine, and heard Dad's voice in my head. 'Just do your best, sweetheart, do it for me.'

Results day was in the autumn, and I'd never been so anxious to log in to my domain to check my results. I almost didn't want to know if I'd passed or failed.

"Merit."

I blinked at the screen in disbelief. I signed out and in again just to be sure, and it was true. I had passed with merit! My heart was thumping quickly as I checked for the third time. I'd done it. I now had a Master's degree!

That was it. I'd had enough of studying and exams. I was satisfied with my academic accomplishments, and finally felt a great weight had been lifted. I felt like I had justified the faith that Mum and Dad had put in me. I felt as if, since losing Dad, all I had done was push myself academically to make him proud. And now at last, I felt as if I'd done that. Now I needed a new goal.

But first, I had my final race of the year – Maidenhead half-marathon.

Within the first mile of the race it began to rain. Then it poured. And it didn't stop.

My T-shirt and shorts were stuck to me in seconds and my hair was plastered to my head.

I couldn't help but wonder why I was doing it to myself. On some level, I thought I must be a tiny bit insane. Why else would I be running 13.1 miles in the pouring rain on a Sunday morning?

As I hit the 11th mile, I was ready to give up, but I forced myself to keep going. By now, I couldn't stop myself thinking of Dad – the thought of him always helped to lift me. And when even that failed, when the pain and the tiredness was almost too much for me, there was always the thought of the medal. I always loved the medals!

I was so grateful that Mum wanted to come and cheer me on, despite the rubbish weather. She stood at the finish line in the town centre, with an umbrella and towel. I was shaking with the cold and tried to warm myself, huddled under a blow-dryer in the ladies' toilets in the town hall. I had to laugh; it was just so ludicrous.

I was so proud of myself on the way home because I'd persevered in such awful conditions and still got a decent race time. I'd surprised myself at how mentally strong I'd been.

But I knew I had still more to give.

I'd been mulling over the possibility of doing a marathon for a while. People kept on suggesting it whenever I told them I ran half-marathons. I dismissed it, thinking there was no way I could ever run that distance. Just over 13 miles was far enough, but double that?! I had no desire to put myself through 26 miles of hell.

There were just too many what ifs:

'What if I need the loo mid-race?'

'What if it's pouring on the race day and I have to do 26 miles in it?'

'What if I collapse from dehydration?'

'What if ... I can't manage the distance?'

Overwhelmed with too many negative thoughts, I kept on shelving the idea.

But slowly, something changed. And that was when all the what ifs turned into a single what if:

'What if I don't try? I'll never know if I can do it.'

I'd finished my studies. I wasn't working full-time. It felt like now was the time to take the plunge and find out just what I was capable of. I was at my peak fitness-wise, and could make it my sole focus for the next few months.

If Dad could do it, why couldn't I?

I remembered seeing the thousands of runners on TV, and a lot of them were much older and larger than me, and in costume – there would probably be a few more dinosaurs in there too. If they could do it …

I went through the motions of researching the best marathons in the UK, but really, there was only one I wanted to do: the London Marathon. Dad had done it in 2 hours 59 minutes the year I was born, so I already had that special connection with it. Plus 2012 was the year London was hosting the Olympics. How fantastic would it be to do the marathon in the city where the Olympic Games were being held?

Places are allocated through a ballot, so there wasn't any guarantee that I'd even get in. I wanted to support a meaningful charity, so I approached Help the Hospices. And I knew that if I could obtain a charity place, it would give me a little extra motivation through the next few months of training. Our local hospice had given us so much support with Dad, and I wanted to do something in return.

I had butterflies as I submitted the application form; my marathon dream was in their hands. Half of me hoped they'd decline my application, so that I wouldn't have to do it, but the other half of me was desperate to secure a place to prove to myself and others that I could do this.

I got the phone call in October, and I was over the moon to hear I'd been successful! They told me they were convinced I was exactly the sort of person they wanted representing them in the London Marathon. I was trembling with excitement as I confirmed I was delighted to accept their offer. I exhaled slowly as I put the phone down – this was really happening. I was now officially running in the 2012 London Marathon and had pledged to raise a minimum of £2000 for the charity.

Now there was just one question: How in the world was I going to raise that amount of money?!

I waited to receive all the paperwork, and the fundraising pack before I told Mum and Natalie. I knew they'd be worried that the distance was too far. But I had prepared answers for all their concerns and tried to convince them that this was a brilliant opportunity to do something exceptional, in memory of Dad. There was a certain irony in that. Dad knew I had hated running when I was young, so the fact that I was about to run in the London Marathon showed I had grown in ways he couldn't have known.

Nothing was going to stop me.

This was it, there was no turning back. My five-month countdown had begun so I wasted no time in getting myself organised and race ready.

The only other person I knew who had run marathons (apart from my dad and my ex-boyfriend's mum) was my godmother, Julia. She'd been in my life since I was a few days old, both as my next-door neighbour and my godmother. I had spent many happy hours playing in the garden with her two sons. Even after she moved, we continued to catch up – and I still call her godmother.

I arranged to meet her as soon as she was free, and told her my big news. She was very proud of me doing something so challenging in memory of Dad, and was thrilled to be able to give me some guidance.

Hearing all her race advice was very reassuring, although the prospect of it – and knowing how much physical preparation I would need – was still very daunting. But the best bit about our catch-up was sharing our experiences of running. We laughed about our black toenails from all the running training, and all our desperate dashes to Portaloos mid-race. I finally had a confidante who truly understood my passion for running, which was so comforting.

We went shopping for running gear and running gels. I'd seen long-distance runners carry these weird pouches of liquid and slurp them mid-race, but I'd never tried one. Nonetheless my godmother was adamant they would help me maintain my energy for the race. Reluctantly I bought a few fruit flavoured pouches and promised to try them out when I trained.

As my godmother hugged me before she left, her final words were, 'Just Do it!' I smiled at her and giggled. The Nike slogan was so very apt for running – and it became our new special phrase whenever we needed to spur each other on. She gave me the self-confidence and belief in myself that I could run the London Marathon and make Dad so very proud.

I invested in new running shoes which were more durable than my usual well-worn race shoes. I devised my own running programme based on ones featured in *Runner's World* magazines and books that I had bought. Saturdays were my long running days, i.e. over 13 miles, while Sundays were my recovery run days. Two days every week, I would do speed and hill training.

I wrote my Saturday running distance programme on a piece of paper and stuck it to my bedroom wall so that I could keep track of my mileage. After my birthday in January, I started to increase my mileage; that gave me three more months to properly prepare.

I was worried about whether I needed to run the full 26.2 miles, but my godmother advised me not to; running that distance would put a lot of strain on my body, and it would take time to recover from it. She recommended running up to 22–23 miles in practice. The final 3–4 miles would be achievable on the day because of the adrenaline. The crowds cheering me on would help see me round, she reassured me. I trusted her, and scheduled in two Saturdays to run between 20 and 22 miles in March so that I had enough time to recover for the big day on 22nd April.

I didn't like the carb gels at all. They were viscous and sickly, and made me feel awful mid-run rather than refuelling me, so I decided to run without them. I also refused to carry any extra stuff like water bottle and iPod; I didn't want to be weighed down and fiddling with stuff while running.

At first, I was able to enjoy the longer runs. The 14 and 15 mile runs came pretty easily to me, but I began to struggle to stay motivated when I ran beyond those. I became bored of my usual routes round the woods and pavements; doing laps was monotonous so I decided to venture further afield and explore the large forest about a mile away. It was ideal because I'd warm up jogging along the pavement to the forest, and then I would distract myself by investigating new routes around it using my watch to measure the time and distance.

Immersing myself in nature and trying to spot deer helped me clock up the miles. I sprinted between lampposts on the way home to increase my speed and get home quicker.

One of the best mind games I used when I felt bored was counting numbers in different languages, in time with my running pace. I began counting 1–50 forwards in English, then backwards, followed by French, Spanish and Chinese. It really made me concentrate, and distracted me from the monotony of running. If I was near a road, I'd tally groups of different cars like white BMWs or new 2012 vehicles, or those with personalised registration plates. It sounds mundane, but I became engrossed in observing passing traffic.

Despite the sub-zero conditions in January, I dragged myself out in the wind, rain and snow. Nothing would deter me from following my running plan. If anything, the more adverse the weather conditions were, the greater the release of endorphins, and the sense of achievement I had.

When I felt like giving up and not bothering with a run, I thought of Dad. And that was the only motivation I needed. At first, I had thought that I had just been doing this race for him, but really it was for both of us.

I tweaked my diet to help fuel my runs and my recovery, and I created new recipes inspired by fitness magazines and books. I swapped white pasta and bread for wholemeal, I fell in love with avocado spread on bagels, and got addicted to blueberries and Greek yoghurt. All these small changes made a huge difference to my stamina. I became leaner and faster. By February I was averaging 40–50miles a week, and transforming into a serious long-distance runner.

The night before my first 20-mile training run, I fuelled up on lots of rice and chicken which I find easy to digest and gives me bountiful energy. I didn't sleep well though, feeling scared that I wouldn't be able to reach my target. I'd heard about runners "hitting the wall" at 20 miles when their bodies shut down and they run out of energy to carry on. Would that happen to me?

It was bright and mild when I set off, pretending to myself that I was only doing 18 miles, so it seemed less daunting. But I chose an extra-long loop round the forest which added two miles. I checked my watch and it flashed "20 miles" I was shocked that I didn't feel more tired. I felt like I was floating and flying. And I was so happy, that I didn't stop when I reached home. With a sudden burst of energy, I did an extra lap round the pond totalling 21 miles! I didn't "hit the wall", I actually felt more physically and mentally stimulated.

With a new sense of confidence, I set myself a finish time target of four hours. With an average half-marathon time of one hour 45 minutes, I decided four hours should be plenty of time to do double the distance. I'd seen some race participants on TV walking the marathon, and taking over seven hours, so I wasn't worried about being slow.

I wanted to complete it in a decent time without walking or stopping though. Doing my best would mean less than four hours. I didn't have the mental stamina or patience for it to take any longer. The faster I reached the finish line the better.

At the end of February though, disaster struck. As I returned from a Sunday recovery run, I felt a blinding pain in my left knee which shot down my whole leg. I nearly fell over as my knee gave way. What had I done to myself?!

I hobbled all the way home, in searing pain. I hadn't tripped and landed badly, so I knew I hadn't broken anything. I just hoped that taking some paracetamol and resting it would help. The knee had gone bright red and swollen, so I followed the "RICE" protocol – rest, ice, compress, elevate. It didn't help much. I had to bite back the tears, and I could barely walk.

What was I going to do now? What about my training schedule? The marathon was just seven weeks away … would I even be able to run?

The doctor thought I had "runner's knee" and suggested I needed to see a physio, but there was a 4–6 week waiting time on the NHS. I couldn't wait that long. Fortunately, there was a private clinic close by, and I managed to get an appointment for the next day.

The physio confirmed the diagnosis of runner's knee. My glute muscles had tightened up because of overtraining. The pain was still unbearable, but the physio prescribed some light exercises in the gym: cycling, squats, lunges and bridge exercises all helped strengthen my body, but running was off the agenda – for at least a week or two. I panicked that I'd lose my fitness and that my months of training would go to waste. But the physio reassured me that I'd be fine, as long as I stopped all high-impact sports until the pain had gone.

Patience had never been my forte, but now I knew I had to rest and let my body recover. Two weeks later, I couldn't stand not running any more, so I tentatively pulled my running gear on, and did a very slow, gentle jog around the pond. The pain came back within a couple of hundred metres, but I persevered. It was still uncomfortable, but it didn't get any worse, and I managed 10k. I was so relieved to get back home in one piece, but it didn't stop me worrying about increasing the mileage. How would I manage 26 miles with that kind of pain?

By the end of March, I was out running again four days a week. My knee was still aching, but I built up the mental resilience to carry on. I decided to do another 21 miler to see how I'd cope with the pain over three hours. It wasn't too bad if I stayed on flat surfaces, but the pain escalated again on undulating routes. I knew that the London Marathon didn't have many inclines, and because I'd done most of my training off-road, I thought that running on tarmac ought to feel a lot easier; I might even be a bit faster.

When I wasn't running I was fundraising. I set up a Facebook page and a JustGiving webpage so that friends and family could watch my progress and donate. The money slowly trickled in over the months, but I was still some way from the £2000 I'd pledged.

To boost my total, I organised an afternoon tea party. I made all the sandwiches and soup, and baked the cakes myself, and all my guests were very generous. Someone even donated £25 for a single slice of Victoria cake!

I contacted my local newspaper, and wrote a press release to promote my story and encourage readers to support my campaign. After my photo appeared in the paper, I had strangers coming up to me in shops, wishing me good luck for the marathon, and donating money.

My stomach did a somersault when I logged in to my donations page to see my total had exceeded £2000! I couldn't believe how many people (especially those I didn't know) had given to my cause and written uplifting messages. I was so touched. More than ever, I knew I had to do it for them now; I felt as if they were counting on me.

By mid-April I was ready. My life had become tedious; all I had done for the past four months was run, refuel, rest, repeat. I just wanted to get out there and go for it before I got injured from overtraining.

The Saturday before the race on Sunday was unbearable. I was fidgety and restless. I had been "tapering" all week (reducing my mileage to stock up my energy reserves) so I was feeling very uncomfortable and dying to do a long run. I knew I shouldn't though, so I cross-trained at the gym and went for long walk to try to feel less bloated.

Three days before the race, I started "carb loading" (eating more carbs at dinner to maximise my glucose levels in the muscles). On Saturday I decided to go for a gentle five-mile jog to loosen my joints and help me relax. It did help, but I was still feeling uneasy about it all. I kept checking the weather forecast for Sunday and we were due to get clear skies and sunshine.

The doubts were creeping in though.

'Had I really done enough training?'

'Would I have the energy to do the extra few miles?'

'What if I was delayed by traffic on my way in to London and missed the start of the race?'

'How would I find Mum at the end?'

I tried to block out the negative thoughts, and ignore all the text messages flying into my phone from well-wishers. I was buckling under the pressure. I was aiming for a sub-four-hour race, but I wondered if I'd been over-confident in my abilities to do it.

In the evening, I laid out all my running gear, and pinned my race number to the yellow vest that Help the Hospices had sent me with "Gem" printed on the front. I knew we had to leave by 6.00am to get to the train station before the road closures, so I had my usual pre-race dinner and went to bed as early as possible.

Unsurprisingly I didn't get much shut-eye. It felt like I was tossing and turning all night long, with race day scenarios playing round in my head. I got up just before 5.00am and had a huge bowl of porridge with a banana. It was freezing, and I was trembling, as I pulled on my tracksuit over my T-shirt and shorts. After we set off, I nearly made Mum turn round and go home because I didn't want to do it. Mum refused.

'Gemma, you've not put yourself and us through all of this for nothing! You are going to do the race and that'll be the end of your running. As soon as it's over, you have to stop running these ridiculous distances.'

For the rest of the journey we remained in silence.

Tears ran down my face as I stared out the window, wishing Dad was driving me. Was I foolish believing I could run a full marathon? Maybe I shouldn't have entered. But now I'd got this far, I didn't want to disappoint him, or any of the people who were supporting me.

I got out of the car at the station and felt completely hollow inside. I didn't want to run. I'd lost my self-belief and motivation.

Mum got out the car because I hadn't budged. It was difficult for her too; I know that now. She coaxed me out, and I melted into a big, firm hug. Very quietly, she reminded me why I was doing this – for Dad and all the others who had sponsored me and were expecting me to do it. I had a duty to fulfil now, whether I liked it or not. Sniffling and blowing my nose, I knew deep down I had to finish what I'd started. I'd come this far, and the end was in sight, albeit 26 miles away!

Mum promised me she'd be at the end on Pall Mall waiting for me, which boosted my spirits.

I thought of Dad. I would be "running in his shoes" along the route. Knowing it would bring me closer to him was the biggest motivation of all. This was the ultimate way to show my love for him.

The train carriages were overflowing with runners. I managed to squeeze on between a couple of burly men wearing pink tutus. There was a buzz in the air, with everyone chatting about their running stories and training. Even though I was among strangers, I oddly felt like we were a team embarking on a big challenge together.

At the other end, there was a fair walk to the lorries to drop off our bags and belongings. The lorries were then driven off to the end of the race, so we could retrieve our things after the ordeal! Such a mammoth task, I had no idea how much preparation and organisation were required. There were dozens of volunteer marshals guiding us to the race village, as well as paramedics on standby. It really began to sink in just how massive this event was. I'd never truly appreciated the scale of it, watching it on TV.

The sun was up now, but it was still cold as I followed everyone else to the running village. I had to pinch myself as I walked around the vast park, with all the TV cameras and reporters. I'd watched it all on TV with Dad, and I couldn't quite believe I was now one of the thousands taking part. With the 9.00am start time approaching, I slotted myself among the hundreds of others and tried to focus, but my heart was thumping hard and fast as the countdown began. I was only dimly aware of the countdown reaching zero, and I shuffled over the start line in a sea of runners.

For the first couple of miles it was very cramped and congested, with people of all ages and nationalities forcing their way through and overtaking each other. The frequent water stations were a nightmare as plastic cups were thrown in all directions. I had to watch my step, hopping over cups and dodging runners weaving in and out of position.

The crowds were five or six rows thick, lining both sides of the streets. Lots of children were waving flags, cheering, and calling out runners' names and numbers. I lost track of how many called out 'Go, Gem!' when I reached 100. Each time I heard someone say my name I smiled and thanked them. I couldn't believe the camaraderie between runners as well. So many patted me on the back encouragingly.

Every mile and kilometre was marked with a huge inflatable, and a digital clock. I found it rather depressing every time I passed one because there were just so many, and I still had so far to go. I needed more ways to distract myself, so I tried to enjoy the sights of London, and looked out for all the funny costumes. How on earth any of them could run as a fully-outfitted Disney character or a London phone box baffled me. It was bad enough running in T-shirt and shorts.

By half way on London Bridge, I was feeling fine, and eagerly looking out for my godmother who said she'd be there wearing a red anorak. Lots of people were wearing red! It was like a game of Where's Wally trying to identify her in the sea of spectators. But suddenly I saw her and yelled out to her, waving madly. She heard me and began jumping up and down giving me the thumbs up. I was so happy to see someone I knew, and it gave me an extra spurt of energy.

By mile 16, the crowds thinned, and the runners dispersed as people began to slow down and tire. I had to push myself to carry on now, because if I slowed, I knew I'd never be able to pick up my pace again. By mile 18, the shooting pain in left knee returned. I was almost reduced to a walk, but I kept going. I was stubborn. I was determined, and I was going to carry on, no matter what.

I couldn't give up months of training. I couldn't let down all the people who'd sponsored me, just because my knee hurt. I thought about Dad, and about how he'd coped without complaining through all his cancer treatment. If he could endure three and a half years of hell, of agony, I could damn well do this!

Mile 22 and heading towards central London – just four more miles to go. This was going to be the real test of my mental and physical stamina. Could I keep up the speed to make my target finish time? I hadn't stopped or drunk anything in three hours, so I was feeling a little light-headed. I didn't want to risk eating or drinking anything because I didn't want to risk aggravating my stomach.

I ignored my body and pushed on. I hadn't hit the wall, but many of the participants I passed had been reduced to walking; some were getting medical help. I felt more driven than ever and convinced that I could do it.

The last few miles were easier than I'd thought. I could feel the sense of anticipation building and it sustained me. I tried to spot any celebrities running or watching the race. Dozens of photographers positioned themselves along the streets, clicking away; I felt famous. Music was blasting, helicopters were flying overhead, people were cheering, the atmosphere was electrifying. It felt like a magnet was drawing me to the finish. I picked up my pace focusing on the best possible finish time.

As I rounded the final corner, seeing Buckingham Palace and the straight, open road towards the end, I was smiling and laughing. I was nearly there! I sprinted as hard as I could, thinking of Dad doing this 23 years ago, and hoped he was watching from above.

800m ... 600m ... 400m ... 200m ... Finish!

I flung myself over the line and heard the mile-marker bleep confirming it was over.

3 hours 35 minutes my watch displayed.

I'd done it! I'd finished well under my target time. I couldn't believe how fast I'd run.

I came to an abrupt halt as soon as I crossed the red finish mats. I was too tired and breathless to say anything. I just looked up to the cloudless sky and thanked my Dad. I couldn't have done it without him inspiring me.

A race marshal gave me a foil cape and goodie bag, while the St John Ambulance staff checked I was okay. I told them I was better than okay, I was flying high! I couldn't stop beaming.

I walked to the finishing area, bustling with reporters, cameramen and the press, looking out for famous people completing the race. Fellow runners kept coming up to me and patting me on the back, congratulating me, and asking about my race time. I simply wanted to absorb everything. It was a once-in-a-lifetime chance, and I wanted to remember it all. I didn't want the feeling to end.

Once I'd gulped down two bottles of water and caught my breath, I staggered over to the lorries lined up further down the road to find my bag and call Mum. She picked up instantly and was ecstatic that I'd finished so soon. We arranged to meet with my godmother by the designated "B" for Bell area, which was jam-packed with families and friends waiting for runners to come through.

I was crying as I saw her and hobbled over as fast as I could. Overwhelmed with emotion I collapsed into her arms. I'd actually run the London Marathon. Just like Dad. My godmother joined us minutes later, equally as excited and proud of me. I didn't want to leave London, the atmosphere was immense, so much happiness and excitement. But Mum wanted me to get home and rest; she was still worried I had pushed myself too hard.

I was stunned that it was over and that I'd survived the 26 miles. As we travelled home in the car, I was too tired to even get changed out of my running gear, so I just wrapped myself up in the foil, and kept hold of the heavy medal. When we pulled up on the driveway, I was almost too weak to get out of the car. My muscles had seized up; I stumbled out with Mum's help. Burning sensations ran down my legs and my feet like nothing I'd ever experienced before.

After a long, hot shower, and dressed in my comfy clothes, I felt refreshed. Hundreds of texts were flooding in from friends and family saying they'd seen me on TV! Natalie had seen me and managed to record it live. I was delighted as she fast-forwarded to my appearance. There I was: a flash of yellow and purple pumping my arms past the camera, metres from the end. How on earth people spotted me in those few seconds was unbelievable, I would have missed it completely.

It was my greatest accomplishment to date, exceeding my degrees or anything else I'd achieved. Aching and sore all over, I climbed into bed, with my medal next to me. My quest to run for Dad was over now. No more ridiculous long runs in freezing conditions. No more black toenails or blisters! I could go back to a "normal" life and relax, couldn't I?

If only it had been that simple.

CHAPTER 9

Running Out of Control

I barely slept the night after the marathon. I woke up in hot sweats, with cramps in my leg muscles, and dizziness from dehydration. I'd never felt so drained, or so uncomfortable.

I felt like this for several days afterwards. I simply had no energy to do anything. For the first time in years I had no desire to run. I was utterly burnt out.

Friends and family kept asking me if I'd become hooked on running – would there be more marathons, or ultramarathons? I laughed. There was no way I could ever run that sort of distance again. I said, 'I'm happy with just doing the one.'

But was I really?

In truth, I was still hooked on running. I kept on competing in half-marathons and pushing myself harder and harder in training. But the marathon started to get more gruelling and more demanding. I started to hate waking up on a Saturday morning, knowing I had to do another monotonous two to three hour run.

I really had only planned to do the one marathon in memory of Dad, and to raise money for charity. I honestly had no intention of carrying on with the ridiculous amount of preparation required for each and every race.

And why would I want to put myself through anything so gruelling ever again?

There weren't any other marathons I wanted to do. My dad had done it, but he hadn't done any others, and I didn't want to spoil the wonderful memories of that special day. I had done my best running, and run faster than ever before, and I knew I'd feel disappointed if I did it again and finished with a slower time. The risk of failing, and of putting all that extra pressure on myself was just too much. I would end my marathon running on a high.

A week later and it still hadn't sunk in that I had completed it. After years of resenting and refusing running, I'd fallen in love with the sport. But now, I was feeling a little lost. I was feeling the post-race blues.

I had nothing else to look forward to. No races lined up. No holiday booked. I didn't have any more studying to do, or a job to go to. I was literally free for the first time in my life. What should I do next?

I've never been one to put my feet up, or go with the flow; I had to have a routine and structure. I had to set goals and reach them.

Running had become an integral part of me. It had given me a sense of freedom and happiness. Even after running in the worst weather conditions, I'd get home, full of adrenaline. And it brought me closer to Dad. If I stopped running, I felt as if I'd be cutting him out of my life again. I didn't want to do that. I didn't want to disappoint him. And I didn't want to forget about running.

As much as I loved running, I needed more structure in my life. I wanted to get the ball rolling with a proper career, like my friends had done, so I chose to focus on that. I'd assumed it would be a doddle securing full-time employment now that I had two degrees, but it wasn't. Competition among graduates was greater than ever, and inevitably I faced numerous rejections which was always disheartening. When I didn't succeed in getting a job, I couldn't help but feel like I'd let Mum and Dad down. They'd used their savings to pay for my private education and I still couldn't get a job to show them it had all been worth it! Guilt-ridden and despondent, I'd go for a run every time the rejections came in.

I was fortunate that Mum let me go on living at home, while I applied for jobs. I just hated feeling like a burden to her. I wanted to be independent and get on with my own life, without feeling like she had to worry about me.

Finally, in August I was offered a role in town planning with a local company. I felt sure that would help me to relax, knowing that, soon, I would have my own income and be able to look after myself.

The only problem was trying to fit in all my training and working a 9–5 job. I couldn't prioritise my running any more, my work took precedence. I had to force myself out of bed in the early hours to cram in an hour's run before work, or else rush to the gym after work, when it would be heaving with other gym goers at peak time. Training became a chore. I wasn't enjoying it that much any more. I was exhausted mentally from work, and paranoid about missing my morning alarm for my pre-breakfast run. I never skipped a session though. Regardless of how drained I felt, I told myself that I would feel far worse if I didn't bother. I didn't want to feel lazy or guilty, so I persevered.

I visualised Mum and Dad watching me while I ran, waiting for me, and smiling as I crossed every finish line. It always motivated me, but it also meant I couldn't stop. I wanted – I needed – to go on doing better and better – for them. I felt as if I had to prove how I was reaching my potential, and how I was exceeding mine (and others') expectations. I wasn't ever competing with anyone but myself. I was running to prove to Mum that my commitment to running was worth it. And, as far as I was concerned, each race demonstrated the progress I'd made.

I'd feel guilty if I didn't perform well because Mum had made the effort to accompany me, and stand around waiting for me to finish, when I know she'd rather have been having a Sunday morning lie-in.

There were times when I absolutely loathed the training and started questioning whether it was worth going on. But when I was in the middle of the race, I couldn't ever imagine a place I'd rather be. I enjoyed it too much; the adrenaline rush I got at the end was better than anything else I did. Running wasn't just a hobby or pastime; it was a lifestyle. I had come too far to give it up, it was a fixed part of my identity. Everyone who knew me would always ask about my running, and they'd be in awe of my achievements. I was worried that if I gave up running, they'd think less of me and I'd lose their admiration. I didn't like being in the spotlight, but I did love getting that validation.

I'd been worried about juggling work and running, but in the end, I just decided I could do it all. Somehow, I had to find a way to excel at both. Lots of people managed it, so I could too. Resolved, I started booking myself in for more half-marathons in 2013 and 2014.

Work was going well, and I found myself rising up the town planning hierarchy. I was as proud as a peacock the day I was promoted and given my first company car. I felt like a real professional, and I had the car to prove it.

All the additional responsibilities and the added pressure at work meant less time to concentrate on running. But, no matter what I did at work, nothing ever seemed to fulfil me as much as finishing a long run. I needed both in my life. But slowly, friends and family had begun to notice that I looked more tired, thinner, less myself, as I carried on pushing myself more in running and working.

At first I was hurt by their comments – no one likes to hear negative things about their appearance. I convinced myself they were just jealous because they couldn't do what I did. So I carried on regardless. I wanted to show them that they were wrong, that I was fit and healthy.

But I didn't. I couldn't. It was as if I had tunnel vision. Running was my priority, and being better every time was my goal. Everything else was secondary.

The more races I ran, the faster I became, and my hunger for success kept on growing. As the months rolled by, my mindset started to change. It wasn't about connecting to Dad any more, I hardly ever thought about him as I ran. It was all about reaching my full potential, and doing my best.

I was now averaging 55–60 miles a week and had no intention of reducing it. I'd come this far, I couldn't bear to think of doing less, or of losing all the mileage I'd clocked up. I didn't care what others thought, or even what I looked like to them. Running made me feel great about myself; it made me feel superior … why would I give up something I loved doing so much?

Running and cross-training at the gym were essential parts of my daily routine, they were non-negotiable. I'd grown so accustomed to exercising every day that it felt unnatural not to do it. I was moody and lethargic until I had done my daily run / gym / bike session. Exercise always energised me and sharpened my senses. I couldn't contemplate life without it.

By 2015, I was prioritising running above everything else. If anything else ever got in the way of my daily routine, it would niggle away at me. I didn't feel I deserved to go out and enjoy myself with my friends and family unless I'd been for a run first. It was never a punishment, I never demonised it. It was guaranteed to make me feel better about myself and gave me something to feel smug about. Only afterwards, would I be able to relax and enjoy my time out, fuelled by the validation I'd got from pushing myself that little bit more.

But other people didn't see it that way. Slowly, more and more people were noticing, and commenting. The most insulting and upsetting comments came from my Chinese grandma. In her basic English she said, 'Gemma, stop running! You very thin and ugly! Not nice pretty girl ...'

Her words pierced me, but I couldn't yell at her because Mum was standing there, and she would have had to defend her mum. I didn't want to start an argument, so I bit back my tears and hurried upstairs so they wouldn't see me cry.

How could she have been so rude to her own granddaughter?! Deep down I knew she loved me, and, on some level, I even knew that she was probably just saying those things because she cared, but in the heat of the moment I hated her for saying it.

I didn't want to listen to or accept people's negativity. They didn't understand how much running meant to me. They didn't run so they couldn't empathise. If they didn't want to support me running, that was their decision. I could carry on without them, just as I had done without William.

I stopped telling friends and family about my races; I didn't need their pessimism. I didn't like adapting my daily routine to suit others, and I feared any change would adversely affect my running. It made me very insular in my thinking. I was convinced my way was the "right and only" way to succeed, and if my family didn't like it, tough luck! I didn't want my life to be controlled by anyone else. I didn't need them to be happy.

When I was feeling low for any reason, I didn't turn to friends for sympathy, and I didn't comfort eat like some people do. I chose to run and, without fail, it made me feel good about myself. It gave me a sense of security, control and happiness. I couldn't rely on anyone or anything else to give me that.

I was overtraining but didn't realise it until I got a stress fracture in my right heel in the middle of a run. It happened so suddenly that I nearly keeled over in agony. I was going downhill in the woods when a shooting pain erupted in my foot, causing my whole leg to feel weak and numb. Somehow, I stubbornly carried on hobbling round so I could finish off the 13-mile route I had planned. I couldn't face stopping and failing.

I was barely shuffling as I reached home, and was crying from the searing pain. What had I done?!

I prayed my foot would stop hurting after some paracetamol and rest that evening, but by the morning it was no better. I got an emergency appointment with my GP but he was no help, just telling me to rest for several weeks. I certainly wasn't going to do that! No way was I going to sit around and do nothing.

At the time I didn't know it was a stress fracture. Nothing showed up on the X-ray, so the doctors assumed it was plantar fasciitis (inflamed muscle on the sole of the foot) or some other strain. I was sure it was something more serious though, so I had a referral to a private consultant. I had an MRI scan for the first time and the images clearly showed a hair-line crack in my heel. The consultant said that I had to stop all high-impact activities to allow the bone to heel – that usually took two–three months.

Feeling downbeat, but satisfied that I knew the cause of my pain, I hobbled back to the car. By the time I arrived home I had already planned my next run. I just needed to know that it would happen. I couldn't bear the thought of going without for too long. There hadn't been a period in my life in the past five years when I had stopped running for more than a few days. I didn't care what the experts said, I was going to continue running.

For the following few days I cycled and went to the gym to reduce the strain on my foot a little bit. But I quickly became bored; the "runner's bug" was always niggling at me. I had to attempt to run again. 'You only fail when you don't try,' I told myself. I was full of optimism when I set out the front door and took a few tentative strides without struggling too much. But it got worse. Less than 100m along the pavement, the blinding pain came back, and I was forced to limp. I was still determined to complete one mile before stopping though, because anything less would have felt so negligible, such a waste of effort.

I kept repeating the same mantra: 'no pain, no gain, it will be worth it!' I wasn't going to be beaten by my own body trying to hold me back from running. I was in so much pain when I hobbled back up the driveway, but pleased as punch with my accomplishment. It was like running for the first time again, just like it had been all those summers ago.

I maintained my reduced running schedule for nearly eight weeks, by which time the pain was more tolerable, so I began to increase the miles again. It was bliss when I went out on my first proper run without being in agony – it made me appreciate how strong my body really was. The sheer pleasure of running felt so intense. I was back up to speed within a couple of weeks and felt much better going back to my old routine.

Mum was worried about my weight and my appearance, and she told me so. She would get fed up of me going for runs and not listening to her advice; she just wanted me to stop it altogether. Maybe she thought I was rebelling, but I wasn't. I never ran to antagonise Mum, I have never wanted to hurt or disrespect her, but the more she put me down, the more I ran to pick myself up. I was locked in a vicious cycle.

Losing weight had never been my intention when I started running because I had already been fit and healthy. I rarely weighed myself, and I'd always been confident about how I looked, without being self-conscious. But with the constant strain I was putting my body under, I had started to notice that my face looked thinner. I was losing muscle tone too. So I just increased what I ate to try to put the weight back on, but it didn't help.

Mum persisted with her scolding whenever I went for a run. I didn't want to fight with her because I knew she was under a lot of pressure. She'd only just started her own catering and café business and had been working flat-out six days a week. I loved Mum so much and hated seeing her stressed and struggling with her business. I wanted to support her, but all I could really do was stay chirpy and be positive for her.

Sometimes though I felt like such a waste of space. No matter what I did to help, it never felt like it was enough to make her happy. The atmosphere in our home didn't feel warm and cosy like it used to. Now it was cold and tense as our relationship disintegrated. And it really was falling apart. No matter how hard I tried, I always seemed to be a disappointment in her eyes.

I tried to strike up conversations about anything at all – even the weather – but she never seemed interested. Most evenings, she didn't even say goodnight to me, but went straight upstairs to her room and shut her door. I felt physically and emotionally cut-off from her. No matter what I did or said to try to reconnect with her, she was unresponsive. Our lives seemed to have diverged and I couldn't find a way to close the divide.

How had our home life become so depressing?

Natalie had moved out to live with her boyfriend so it was just me and Mum in the house, and I felt completely alone. I chatted to Natalie on the phone weekly, but I tried to avoid talking about running, or about Mum because I didn't want her to worry about us. I didn't want to escalate the problem further.

Mum finally broke her silence one Saturday lunchtime after I returned from my usual long run. She absolutely exploded, and threatened to throw me out of the house if I didn't get help, because she was at the end of her tether. She said she couldn't live with me and my rigid routine any more; it was impossible for her to enjoy my company – and my running was the cause of it.

I stood, in my running gear, in complete silence as I let her vent. When she had finished, she marched into her bedroom and slammed the door, while I remained rooted to the spot. The endorphin rush from my run instantly evaporated as her words rang in my ears.

I was overwhelmed with guilt as she blamed me for ruining our relationship. Suddenly, I didn't feel worthy to be her daughter. It seemed like she had stopped loving me.

For the rest of the day I let it all turn over in my head. I tried to look at things from her perspective, and finally decided I needed to do something. I needed to take the plunge and seek medical help. It wasn't just me that needed healing; it was our relationship. I couldn't stand the tension in the house any more and was fed up of feeling like an outcast because of my running.

Later, we had a calm discussion about what I was going to do. I agreed to try Cognitive Behavioural Therapy (CBT) which she thought would help with my "addiction to running". She embraced me and said she would support me through it all. It was the first time in ages that I felt like she really cared. Her hug felt so wonderful.

I hated myself for making Mum angry, it made me feel wretched with myself. I wanted to show that I was being co-operative, and that, if my running was a problem, I could control it.

I was still sceptical about how beneficial the CBT was going to be. I'd always associated it with people who had serious mental conditions, and I didn't think that was me. But I went along, having promised Mum I'd try it.

From the first session I found the therapist very patronising and intimidating. She would interrogate me about every aspect of my life and claimed that I was punishing myself. I found that ludicrous. Why would I be punishing myself? Surely my running was the exact opposite – it was one of the few enjoyments I had left in my life. I ended up having heated arguments with her and going in circles, discussing the same topics again and again, and constantly defending myself.

I listened to what she said but I wasn't persuaded she was right. I refused to be told what to do, especially by someone who didn't know me personally and wasn't a runner. She couldn't empathise with my situation.

Now that I reflect back on the sessions, I realise that therapists are supposed to be impartial. They don't get involved with their clients' stories, so I feel that my approach, and my expectations were wrong at the time. And that's why the therapy wasn't very effective. I wasn't open-minded enough. I didn't want to be told I was wrong.

I understand now that the point of CBT is for the therapist to encourage the client to explore and figure out for themselves how and why they got to that mental state. The therapist probes their clients to get them to dig deep into their past to allow underlying issues to surface. Only then can the client and therapist work together on moving forward and untangling the problem. Back then, I was just too impatient, I didn't feel like I could reveal all of my personal history to a stranger.

I wanted a quick fix to my problems and became disillusioned when I didn't feel as if I was progressing at all. I was getting nowhere, and felt worse after an hour with her than I did before attending the session. She was making me feel guilty about myself and demonising running.

Each week I put up with the same message – I had to stop running if I wanted to move forward in life and mend things with my mum. That was out of the question. I wasn't prepared to give it all up. There had to be another solution. At the end of two months of CBT, I decided to stop. I was getting more and more miserable and, as a result, running even more to lift my spirits.

I was beginning to feel as if I had no one to turn to. Nobody understood.

I didn't want to tell my godmother, Julia, about my struggles with running, or about the CBT because I just felt too ashamed. I didn't even talk to Natalie about my insecurities. She hated running and wouldn't have been able to understand why I ran nearly every day. I was too proud to admit to her that CBT hadn't worked.

I didn't want to show any weaknesses. I never had. I was supposed to have everything under control. How could I reveal to her that I was an emotional wreck? I was afraid to hear what she'd say. I was worried she'd take Mum's side when I felt like I needed her sympathy so much. I didn't want her to tell me to get counselling, or any other kind of help, because I still didn't want to accept that something was wrong with me.

I had never failed at anything, so I didn't tell her about my CBT. To admit that I was struggling, or that my relationship with Mum was broken was unthinkable to me. And if Natalie did ask, I'd just change the subject in a false cheery voice to hide my anxiety.

Once, I had been able to talk to her about anything without ever feeling embarrassed or judged, but now I felt I had to distance myself to protect myself. I didn't want to cry and break down on the phone to her. I didn't want her or anyone to know that I wasn't coping.

Each day was the same as the one before: it was an endless cycle of work and exercise. I stopped entering races because I'd done all the local ones, and my heart just wasn't in it any more. I had stopped looking forward to them now that Mum no longer supported my passion. The last time I had asked, she'd told me it was a waste of time waiting around for me to finish, and I was crushed to hear that.

It wasn't much fun driving myself to the one remaining race I had booked. And I didn't run as fast, knowing she wouldn't be there, eagerly looking out for me at the finish line. I had no one to congratulate and hug me at the end. I felt awkward as other runners celebrated with their family and friends. I had to sheepishly ask a stranger if they could take a photo of me with my camera, just so that I had a memorable picture of me at the finish with my medal.

When I arrived home, still full of endorphins, Mum didn't ask how I'd done. She just carried on doing whatever household chore she was in the middle of. I stomped upstairs tired from the race and deflated from her lack of interest. I tried to feel my pride in the moment as I hung my new medal on the wall among the dozen others, but I didn't really feel it inside.

I felt entirely disconnected from all my friends and family, it was as if I was just existing rather than actually living my life. I turned down invitations to socials and parties because I was too self-conscious about the way I looked. I didn't want friends to tell me how thin I looked. I didn't want to hear the truth. I couldn't face people staring at me and whispering about me making me feel even more insecure. Excluding myself that way helped me to go on feeling "safe" in my own little bubble.

I suppressed all my emotional pain and numbed myself by being constantly busy, staying out of the house as much as possible. Running was my escapism, but it sometimes felt as if I was running in a maze, desperately trying to find a way out but constantly hitting dead-ends. No matter which way I turned, I was lost.

My running came to a sudden halt in the autumn of 2015.

I was riding home on my bike, ready to signal my exit left from a roundabout, when I heard a car zooming behind me. I could sense that it was trying to overtake, but suddenly felt the full force of it as it collided into me. I was flipped straight over my bike, landing heavily in the middle of the road. For the next few moments I didn't know what had happened as I lay motionless on the tarmac. Strangers suddenly crowded round, shouting at me to make sure I was still alive. The driver had also stopped; she was screaming and shouting at me in a foreign language.

My breath had been knocked out of me, so I couldn't speak at first. The searing pain from my left knee was blinding. I knew something wasn't right straight away; I couldn't move it.

My helmet had saved my head from smashing into the ground, and I could move all my other limbs, apart from my left knee. I heard the sirens in the distance, and my heart sank as I knew they were coming for me. I had never watched medical TV series because I don't like all the blood and gore, but now I felt like I was in one of them as I saw the flashing lights pull up next to me and the medical team get out with a stretcher.

I was sobbing. 'I don't want to go to hospital, I'll be fine. I've got to get home, where's my bike? Is it okay?'

The paramedics, two women, were very patient and gentle and as they checked me over for any life-threatening injuries. I was shaking, petrified that there was something seriously wrong. Had I broken or fractured something? Would I need an operation?

Once it was established it was only my knee that needed medical attention, I began to panic. 'I can't go to hospital, I've got work tomorrow, and a half-marathon next weekend ... what will I tell my mum? She'll be livid ...'

I wanted them to stitch my knee at the roadside and drop me off home, but the laceration was so large and deep that I needed go to A & E immediately. Sirens blaring, lights flashing, they rushed me off to hospital. Sitting up in the ambulance, I gazed down at the gory sight. The skin on my knee had been completely torn away and blood was spilling everywhere.

'God! Why did this have to happen to me?!'

The police had arrived and were speaking to the driver to get a statement. They spoke to several eye-witnesses to try to establish who was at fault, and then, when the paramedics had calmed me down, I was able to give my version of the incident. I was convinced the driver was to blame but the police officers said it would take several weeks to review the evidence.

There was nothing I could do but accept her insurance details and try to make a claim for the damage to my bike – and my own injuries. (A few months later I found out that because there wasn't any film-footage showing what had happened, they couldn't determine who was at fault. The driver was only given a police warning and was required to go on a Driving Awareness course. That was it! No fine, no driving licence points deducted, no criminal charges. My case was closed.)

In that moment though, all I could think about was what was going to happen to me. My heart sank as I bumped along in the ambulance and everything began to sink in.

The last time I'd been to a hospital was when my dad had been having cancer treatment. This wasn't the same place, but I still felt uneasy as I was wheeled into the A & E department and given a bed while I waited for the nurses to assess my knee.

It felt like hours until I was seen, and I was desperate to get home. They gave me a local anaesthetic to numb the area around the laceration and stitched it back together. I couldn't watch the nurse passing the needle in and out of my skin and pulling the threads tight.

It was a complete mess. It needed nearly 20 big stitches to seal the wound. They bandaged it to keep it clean and I wasn't allowed to get it wet until the stitches were taken out 10 days later ...

What?! *Ten* days! How was I going to shower? More importantly, how was I going to run?

In the end, I had to call Mum to come and get me and my damaged bike. I was so relieved to see her after my traumatic day. I was worried she would yell at me, but she was just glad I was alive, given what had happened.

The anaesthetic wore off quickly and by early evening I was in agony. I could hardly move because of the intense pain. I had no appetite. I couldn't wash or do anything that I would normally be able to do. I had no motivation. I just slumped on the sofa and cried. I felt as if my world had fallen apart. How was I ever going to recover from this? When would I be able to run again?

I took sick leave from work and felt like an even bigger burden to Mum.

Once the stitches were taken out of my knee, I was scared the skin would rip open. But when that didn't happen, I knew I had to make up for lost time.

Some people probably wouldn't get back on a bike if they'd had an accident like that, but I was determined to overcome my fear. I got my bike fixed and by the end of the fortnight I was cycling again on designated cycle paths. I wasn't brave enough yet to go back on the roads.

I tentatively set off for a run less than three weeks after the incident, and although my knee ached with each step I took, I managed several hundred metres. It wasn't much, but something was better than nothing and it was reassuring to be back to more-or-less full health.

In early December I resumed with my training schedule. I was still quite weak from the accident, and my body hadn't recovered from the ordeal, but I didn't want to rest, I wanted to run. Regardless of the dreary weather, I set off for my usual Saturday morning long run.

I didn't feel quite right. I was shivering throughout the run and it was more of an effort than usual. I started feeling breathless, which was unlike me. I was aiming for 11–12 miles but by 10 miles, I struggled to place one foot in front of the other. I was gasping, taking more and more short, stuttering breaths.

I should have stopped. I needed to stop. But I couldn't. 'Come on, Gem, what's wrong with you? You've done this hundreds of times before, keep on going!'

The harsh wind was blowing against me and slowed me even more, so eventually, I decided to head for home. My vision was getting blurry, making it hard to find my way. I reached my front door, gasping for breath, and stumbled into the house.

I felt dizzy, but assumed it was just because I was so cold. I thought I'd warm up with a hot shower. As I tried to climb the stairs, I lost my balance and tripped. I clung on to the bannister and eventually got to the top and shuffled into the bathroom. Getting undressed and clambering into the bath, my whole body trembled as I swayed under the shower head. The hot water did nothing to warm me up. I couldn't even hold the shampoo bottle because I was shaking so much.

I didn't know what was happening.

I gave up trying to wash my hair and turned the shower off before reaching for my towel and wrapping it around me. I crouched down to step out of the bath tub onto the bath mat, holding on to the glass shower door. I didn't have the strength to dry myself with the towel, and just stood there shivering and dripping wet.

Suddenly everything went out of focus. I could only see black and white. I tried to sit down on the toilet seat to steady myself, but I slipped and fell on the floor.

I couldn't hear or see anything. I didn't have the energy to shout. I reached out, desperately scrambling to try to find something to grasp onto, but I couldn't.

And then everything went black.

CHAPTER 10

'It's All my Fault!'

'Where am I? I'm cold ...'

I could hear the sirens. They were blaring in my ears. Somebody was staring down at me. I didn't know who it was.

'Mum, help! What's happening?'

The figure looking down at me said, 'Gemma, can you hear me? You're in an ambulance. Your mum is here. Please don't move. Are you in any pain?'

I was lying on an uncomfortable stretcher with just a few blankets on me. My hair was damp, and I was shaking violently.

Where was I going? Not hospital, please not hospital!

'Gemma, you've had a bad fall, and we're taking you to hospital. How do you feel?'

'I'm very cold, my body aches,' I stuttered.

I felt Mum come over and hold my hand, but I kept drifting in and out of consciousness. It wasn't until I was transferred to a ward hours later that I felt more alert. By now, I was dressed in a thin, itchy hospital gown with an identity tag on my wrist.

I was in an acute dependency ward with nine other, mostly elderly, patients. Young nurses whisked between the beds tending to us. I had tubes connected to my head and chest monitoring my every movement.

I was terrified. It felt as if dozens of nurses and doctors were attending to me. They were setting up a blood transfusion and injecting me with essential minerals to help strengthen me. Nothing felt real.

As the hours passed, I fell in and out of fitful sleep. I didn't have the energy to sit up, let alone walk to the toilet. I was forced to use a commode – which was mortifying for me.

Lying flat on my back completely helpless, all I could think about was what an idiot I had been to end up here.

I turned my head and saw Mum perched on a seat next to me. Her eyes were wide open, barely blinking, clearly in shock.

The words rushed out of me. 'I'm so sorry, Mum. I can't believe I'm here … I've let you down. I hate myself. I don't want to be here. I'm sorry that I've put you through all this …'

Mum stroked my head and held my hand, trying to reassure me that everything would be alright.

She filled in the blanks for me. She told me how she'd found me unconscious on the bathroom floor late in the afternoon. She thought I was dead. In desperation, she had called for an ambulance. All she could do was hold on to my limp body and pray that it wasn't too late to save me.

I couldn't tell her how grateful I was that she'd found me. I was overwhelmed with guilt and kept apologising for scaring her. It was never my intention to try to kill myself.

The paramedics had saved my life. They had resuscitated me in the ambulance on the way to the hospital.

Mum told me how much she loved me, and that Natalie and I would always be the most important people in her life. Hearing her say that made my heart melt, and I felt even guiltier for what had happened. In that moment, I knew she really was the best mum in the world. She had been through such hell with losing Dad, and then everything that had happened with me. I owed her so much. How could I make it up to her?

We waited for what seemed like hours for the duty doctor to visit me and tell me what was going to happen next. I was expecting to be discharged so that I could go home and watch *Strictly Come Dancing*.

'What time can I leave?' I enquired.

'I'm sorry, Gemma, but you'll be staying here for at least a day or two, because you are very unwell. You passed out earlier today due to low blood sugar and body weight. You're very lucky to be alive. Most people wouldn't have made it. We need to keep you here to monitor your progress until we feel you're strong enough to return home.'

'But I don't want to sleep here! I haven't got any of my things, I haven't showered, I don't want to be surrounded by all these people ...' I began to cry. 'You can't keep me here!'

Mum had to comfort me and reassure me that it was for the best. She told me I'd be home in no time. She hugged me tightly and promised to come for me in the morning.

There was nothing I could do. I could barely stand, let alone walk out of hospital. I felt like an invalid.

There was a washroom at the end of the ward and a nurse kindly helped me shower and get changed. It calmed me down and helped me feel a little less grotty.

I didn't sleep at all. I had agonising cramps in my leg muscles and kept needing the toilet due to the vast amount of fluids they forced into me. The ward was noisy with patients being wheeled in on beds throughout the night. The night nurses swished around routinely checking up on me and checking my blood pressure and sugar levels.

A nurse came and took blood every hour. As I looked down at my bruised arm, sore from all of the needle-pricks, it struck me just how thin I was. I could see my veins protruding. I hadn't noticed that before. I didn't recognise my own body.

In the morning, I shuffled to the washroom, dragging the machine I was now permanently attached to with me. I looked at myself with disgust in the mirror. My hair was straggly and limp, my cheek bones angular and visible and the hospital gown hung loosely over my emaciated limbs.

I hardly recognised the painfully gaunt woman staring back at me. 'What have I done to myself?'

This was all my fault. I had let my running get out of control! I had worn my body out. I should have listened to Mum when she had begged me to stop. I should have listened when my body was telling me I was overdoing it! That's why I'd got a stress fracture; my body hadn't been coping, and I'd just ignored it!

My life had been reduced to sleeping, eating and running. That was all I had. It sounded so stupid and pathetic! It wasn't a life at all. I had never felt like that about myself. I had always been so healthy, strong and confident. The fun and colour of life that I had worked so hard to find had all drained away. Everything was monochrome.

I knew I had to recover for my own sake, and my mum's. We couldn't carry on as we had been, living separate lives in the same house, avoiding speaking to each other. She didn't have to save my life to make me understand she loved me; I knew she did. And I knew I had to do this for her. I had to show her I was willing and able to change.

Back in my bed, a tray had been left with my breakfast. It reminded me of being in a hotel: a little glass of orange juice, a selection of small packets of cereal, and fresh fruit, yoghurt and rolls with butter. I was ravenous so ate most of it before the doctors and consultants arrived mid-morning to assess me.

As promised, Mum arrived just after breakfast and we waited for the consultants to come to my bed. They decided that my body weight was still too low. I couldn't be trusted to look after myself, the doctors said. I couldn't go home.

I tried to convince them that I was fine; I told them I knew that it was my fault for running too far on Saturday. I felt stronger already, and I knew I could reach a safe weight at home, but they were adamant. I was staying in hospital, and I would be there until I reached a safe weight. I'd put my body through a lot, and they needed to ensure I was being fed safely. They moved me onto a less critical ward and gave me a nurse 24/7 to help me.

I didn't feel like I needed a nurse, I was perfectly capable of doing things (very slowly) by myself, but I had no choice. If I refused to co-operate then I could have been sectioned under the Mental Health Act.

There was nothing I could do but follow their instructions. I realised that arguing wouldn't help. I turned to Mum for support, but she was firm with me. She said this was the fastest way to get better and be discharged. And deep down, I knew that was right. I'd refused help in the past – and I'd ended up in hospital. I needed support now.

I cried for ages in Mum's arms as I resigned myself to the fact that I was going to be stuck there indefinitely. It felt like the ultimate punishment for my "addiction" as Mum had called it. There was nowhere I could run to now, though. Nowhere to hide. I had to face my fear of change in order to become healthy again.

I got a bed by the window in the new ward, with an uninspiring view of another concrete building. I gazed outside wishing I could breathe in fresh air and be enjoying the festivities like everyone else. It was two weeks until Christmas. Surely I would be home before then?

I was wrong.

After more consultations with numerous doctors, it was decided I would have to remain in hospital for a few weeks until I was mentally and physically stable.

I was going to spend the festive season alone, unable to celebrate with my family and friends. I couldn't even tell any of my friends I was in hospital because I didn't want them to see me looking so dreadfully ill. I was too proud. I had always thought of myself as a high achiever, but now ...

I didn't want to be judged or pitied by friends. They wouldn't understand, nobody would.

I clock-watched constantly. The time dripped by at a snail's pace. I found it difficult to distract myself. Every day a new nurse would sit with me and escort me to the bathroom in case I fell. Even at night, a nurse would be there next to my bed as I attempted to sleep. It was a strange and uncomfortable way to sleep, knowing that a stranger was staring down at me as I lay there.

Bed rest was mind-numbingly boring but essential to regain my strength. I never used to weigh myself but in hospital it was done every morning before breakfast. I didn't want to know exactly how much I weighed. Just to be told that it had gone up was all I cared about.

I was assessed by the in-house mental health team and they concluded that I didn't have an eating disorder or any other serious mental health issues. So that meant I didn't have to see any counsellors or therapists. They were happy that I could be discharged as soon as I reached that safe weight.

I was forced to have a food tube inserted up my nose and down my throat so I could take on extra liquid calories to speed up my recovery. That only made me look even more hideous, and I had to wheel my feeding machine around with me everywhere.

The doctors were worried that the food tube kept moving around in my stomach. Subsequently I had to go for X-rays to make sure it wasn't doing me any damage. The hospital was extremely busy so I would often be woken up at 3.00am – it was the only time when they had a free time slot. It was strange and disorientating to be woken up in the middle of the night and be told I needed to have an X-ray.

There were times when I just felt like nothing was ever going to change. And times when I wondered how I'd got into that state. I hadn't done anything wrong, I had only wanted to push myself a little further, just a little further. Why was I being put through all of this?

The days revolved around meal times and medical observations (obs) when they'd check my blood pressure and take bloods. The regimented timings made it feel like being back in school, with set meal times: breakfast at 8.30am, lunch at 12.30pm, and dinner at 6.30pm. Obs were done at 7.00am, 11.00am, 4.00pm and 9.30pm. Visiting hours were 10.00am to 8.00pm and then bed was 10.00pm. But I lost track of the days; they all blended into one another.

The other patients in my ward seemed to sleep all day, so I was very lonely. During the day I wrote my private thoughts in a notebook. It wasn't just so I could reflect on what had happened; I wanted to figure out how I was going to solve this.

I had a sinking, guilty feeling in my stomach as I thought everything through. I could have prevented it. If I hadn't run so much; if I hadn't over-trained, then I wouldn't have ended up in hospital. My body had been telling me to stop, and I had ignored it. Even when I'd had a bad injury, I'd forced myself to keep running. My body had stopped coping, and I'd gone on pretending that everything was okay.

I had been too proud – or too afraid – to vocalise my concerns. I had wanted to be invincible and not worry my family and friends. But I recognised then that I had become addicted to running because it gave me a sense of control over my life. Without Dad I still felt lost, but I knew that having a strict routine at least helped me to feel secure. Running and exercise produced endorphins and helped me feel great about myself when I was feeling anxious or depressed. It made me feel as if I could escape reality, and free myself from life's hardships.

Home life had become so difficult. Mum was so stressed about everything: her business, taking care of her mum, our financial concerns … She was exhausted and disillusioned with it all and I hated seeing her going through all of that. I couldn't stop hoping and wishing that Dad was still with us. He had been the one who had taken care of all our worries in the past. He had been Mum's rock, her shoulder to cry on, her best friend, the love of her life …

It crushed me when I thought about her life; about everything that she was still going through, without Dad.

And I wondered what he would think of me now … His own daughter had ended up in hospital. All because I had wanted to follow in his footsteps.

If he hadn't died, would I still have become obsessed with running? I could never have blamed Dad for what had happened. But I felt like I would always be angry at the cancer that had killed him.

I wasn't trying to replace Dad, but I wished I could have comforted and supported Mum more so that she could enjoy her life. I felt like a burden living at home; no matter how much I had wanted to make things better in our relationship, I couldn't.

She had tried so hard to stop me overtraining, but I had never listened. I felt like a failure because CBT hadn't worked. I had always thought that I knew what was best for me. Perhaps I had become too self-absorbed in my own "safe" bubble that I rejected others' opinions. The truth hurt, and perhaps I was a coward for not being able to face it.

God, I hated myself for making such a mess of things!

But I knew that I still had a chance to make things right.

I wrote 'Actions speak louder than words' in my notebook. I knew I had to physically change and not just say that I wanted to change if I really wanted to move forward with my life.

Everything that had happened had been a shock to Natalie too. I was ashamed when she arrived at the ward, because she hadn't seen me like that before. She was visibly overwhelmed by everything that had happened. She had no idea how serious my running obsession had become and was crying as she saw me lying in bed.

I was genuinely touched by her love for me, and relieved that she was there to help me get through it all. It seemed ridiculous that I had hidden all my struggles from her in order to appear in control, and better than her. I was tired of competing, and at that moment in time I needed her encouragement to overcome this battle.

Without fail, Mum or Natalie came every afternoon and kept me company for an hour or so, chatting about what was happening out in the real world. Seeing them was the highlight of my day. I cherished every minute with them and tried to make the most of our time together. They always did their best to lift my spirits. I wouldn't have coped without them. Even at dinner times …

The dinners were exceedingly unappetising. When the trays of food arrived, they reminded me of aeroplane meals. I craved proper home cooking, so Mum offered to cook and bring in her chicken, broccoli and rice that I used to love as a little girl. The hospital staff just wanted me to eat and regain my strength, so I enjoyed tucking into hot, familiar food every evening. It felt like such an important token of her love for me.

During the day I would be wheeled out into the hospital courtyard for some fresh air with my nurse, and I savoured that half-hour of freedom from the ward. I closed my eyes, listened to the birds, and transported myself away from the hospital. It made me appreciate how much I'd taken the simple things in life for granted.

I had no urge to run while I was in hospital. I was too weak, and my body ached all over. I didn't have the strength to do any physical activity at all. I wasn't even sure if I would ever be able to run again. And after everything that had happened, I wasn't sure if I wanted to. I still felt that I despised myself for letting it rule and almost ruin my life. I didn't ever want to let it happen again.

I thought about Dad, and about how he had no control over the cancer which ultimately killed him. But I did have control over this. It wasn't like cancer, I was free to live my life, and I knew I needed to respect my body more.

I knew then – more than ever – that life was precious. I finally recognised that there was so much more beyond running. I had spent so long concentrating on being the best runner, but my strict regime had got me nowhere in life.

How stupid had I been to let my life become so one dimensional? At a distance, I could see that compelling myself to run ridiculous distances had become so meaningless. In pursuit of that adrenaline rush, I had shut off everyone I loved, and shut down any other areas of enjoyment in my life.

I wanted that chance to get better and get back to the person I'd been before running: the fun-loving daughter, sister and friend.

Determined to get released as soon as possible, I stuck to the dietician's and doctors' orders, and as a reward for doing so well, I was permitted a few hours' leave from hospital on Christmas day. It was the best present I could have wished for.

That short time at home with Natalie and Mum was spent opening our presents and watching some silly Christmas TV together. Mum and Natalie had decided that it would have been unfair to decorate in the usual way because I wouldn't be home long enough to celebrate properly. It didn't matter though.

The few special hours away from the hospital were all I needed to give me the boost I needed to get well and return home for good.

On Boxing Day, my godparent came to visit me. At first, I was embarrassed about telling her, but she was so sympathetic. As a nurse, she was completely at ease in the ward, so she didn't stare or interrogate me about all the different drips and machines I was attached to. It was refreshing being treated like a "normal" person and not like a patient. Chatting non-stop about all the things happening in the wider world made me miss my freedom even more. It was another reminder that there was so much more to embrace in life beyond the confines of the hospital. I really felt that I was loved by others who just wanted me to get better.

'Just do it!' she whispered to me as she tightly hugged me goodbye. 'You show them girl, you can do this!'

I wasn't trying to battle on my own any more. And now that I was accepting help from others, I finally started to feel as if I was making progress, and there was no reason why I couldn't continue to get better. I waved goodbye to her, feeling confident that I could and would recover.

CHAPTER 11

Running Towards the Light

The day dawned bright and sunny on 4th January 2016, and I hoped it would be a positive sign that I was going to be discharged. I was due to meet the consultants to hear their verdict, and was praying that they would allow me to go home for good.

I was feeling much stronger and more myself again, especially because I didn't need a nurse sitting with me 24/7. I sat up in bed waiting impatiently for my last obs – and the results were normal, thank goodness.

A nurse also silenced the annoying bleeping from the machine I was attached to. My final food drip had finished hours ago, and it was bleeping to let everyone know. Now that I was unchained from it for the first time in weeks, I could finally walk around without dragging the cumbersome thing along with me.

I busied myself all morning trying not to clock-watch. I couldn't wait to get home for some proper peace and quiet. The constant racket on the ward made it impossible for me to rest. I'd had no privacy apart from a thin curtain that could be drawn around my bed in the evening.

My godmother came to keep me company, and she was delighted at the progress I'd made in the time since she'd seen me.

I was given a few hours' leave before my consultant's meeting, so she took me for a drive to get away from the depressing hospital environment for a bit. I discovered I was still quite weak as I struggled to get in and out of the car, but I refused any assistance. I wanted to show I was capable of looking after myself.

We went for a short stroll in the woods where I used to run. It was still frosty with icicles dangling off the fir trees and the tundra ground was glistening with dew drops. My wellie boots were still the only footwear I could slip on over my puffy ankles, but they were ideal for these cold conditions. My senses became alive when we immersed ourselves in nature. Smelling the fresh pine and breathing in the chilled air really transported me away from the gloom of hospital and reminded me of the simple pleasures of life that I had forgotten. Hearing my favourite birds set my heart aglow, and I thought about Dad. I knew I'd let him and Mum down, and that still hurt. But I'd let myself down too.

We passed several dog walkers, luckily no one I recognised. I was very self-conscious about my gaunt appearance and the food tube hanging around my face, so I wasn't keen on bumping into neighbours.

Back at the ward, my godmother held my hands and looked me in the eye and said, 'You know what I'm going to say … just do it! You show them that you can! You've got your whole life ahead of you, and so many things to look forward to, so seize this chance!' I beamed back and promised I would!

I was shaking with nerves as I followed the consultants into a tiny, cramped room. I felt as if I was awaiting a hearing at the High Court in Westminster, with all the senior medical staff staring at me intensely. I held my head up high though and smiled throughout, determined to prove that I was healthy enough to be discharged.

It was a short meeting. I had exceeded my target weight, and the blood tests showed that my body was functioning normally again.

They were letting me go home.

The news sent my heart flying. I almost leapt out of my seat and jumped for joy but thought it was more sensible to remain calm and not overexert myself. In just a few hours I would be home for good! I had done it!

Everyone was very pleased with my progress. They recognised that I didn't have an eating disorder, and could see that I had obeyed their instructions without any problems. They were confident that I was no longer a threat to myself. But they wanted to ensure I carried on gaining weight safely, and didn't revert back to my dangerous old habits after being discharged hence I was referred to an eating disorders clinic as an outpatient.

I was straight on the phone to Mum. She was thrilled for me, and came straight round to take me home. I wasn't the least bit sad packing up my belongings. I was grateful for what all the staff had done to help me, but I'd had enough of being in captivity. I couldn't stand being treated as an invalid any more, I was ready to interact with the rest of society, and feel a part of it.

Having the food tube removed from my nose and throat was the best part. It was bliss being able to swallow properly and wash easily without the tube swinging in the way. Just before I left the hospital, the identity band was cut from my wrist, and finally I felt like I had been released from prison.

I had a spring in my step as I walked arm-in-arm with Mum. As we crossed the threshold of the hospital to the car park, I didn't look back. This was a moment to be proud of for the rest of my life. I was no longer a critically ill patient, but a positive young lady about to embark on a new era of my life.

My first night back at home went by quickly. It was only the morning after, when I shakily sat up in bed, that I realised how much of a physical challenge it was going to be doing everything by myself. In hospital, I'd had the assistance of an automatic airbed to help me sit up and then stand after sleeping. My own flat mattress was far more comfortable, but difficult to roll out of.

After several minutes of heaving myself up, I shuffled to my cosy bathroom and then hesitated when I got there. I had a sudden flashback of the day I collapsed. I was a little scared of it happening again. I was completely alone, Mum had left for work, so I knew I had to be extra careful. But I was determined to get clean; I didn't want to smell like a patient any more.

I had a long hot shower, washed my hair, and made sure that I climbed in and out of the big bath tub very carefully! I felt bizarrely chuffed with myself for achieving something that would have been so straightforward for most people, but felt like a real confidence booster for me.

Everything took so much longer than it should have done. I was used to bounding up and down the stairs in seconds, but to begin with, I had to tentatively cling on to the bannister as I took each step. Doing everyday chores like washing or putting the rubbish out were far more tiring than I had expected. Things became easier over the next few days as my ankles settled down. As I got much more mobile, I was able to go walking in the woods again.

I drove myself to the eating disorder clinic once a week to a see a consultant. I felt completely out of place as I wandered to reception on my first visit. It was a dark, dated building, and felt very depressing.

My consultant told me about what the centre did for patients diagnosed with mental illnesses and eating disorders, and it really put things into perspective for me. I couldn't comprehend how or why so many young people ended up hating themselves and punishing themselves to such an extent. But I knew people might have said that that was exactly what I'd done.

It was quite emotional, and I was choked up as some of the inpatients were escorted to a communal dining room. A few were crying and rebelling as the staff did their best to comfort them as they guided them into the room.

I never ever wanted to end up in hospital again; I didn't want to abuse my body like I had before. I'd put myself and my family through enough hell over Christmas. There was no way I would go back to my old ways! I cherished the prospect of the life I could now lead.

My meetings with the consultant were straightforward, and as the weeks passed, he was impressed by my consistent weight increase. Each time I saw him I became more self-assured and "radiated confidence," he said.

It was true. The more time I spent at home, the more I appreciated how my time in hospital had been the ultimate wake-up call. Having spent so many weeks restricted to bed rest I knew that nothing bad would happen to me just because I wasn't doing strenuous exercise. I had benefited mentally and physically for letting myself relax and recover, and I intended to continue doing so. I discovered that I did have the inner strength to adapt and change.

In the past, I had manged to channel all my mental and physical energy into achieving my goals, whether that be academic or sports-related. Now I needed to use my willpower and strength to make the changes in my life to become better, healthier and happier.

I knew I had it in me. I had to "just do it!" as my godmother always said.

New habits take a while to bed in, so I knew I would feel uneasy at first. I didn't like feeling out of control, and I missed having the same sort of structure in my life that running had given me. So I just kept telling myself that the more I put myself in uncomfortable situations and tested my boundaries, the more I would improve and grow as a person.

A month later and the consultant was satisfied with my progress and discharged me from the centre. I was over the moon. It felt like proof that I was well on my way to leading a normal life again. It was the last piece of the jigsaw – the boost I needed to push myself into a new phase of life.

I began to wake up each morning feeling freer. Not pressurising myself to run was liberating. For the first time in years I was behaving like a "normal" person again. I'd forgotten what it was like to live a life that wasn't dictated by sports. I wasn't a professional runner. It suddenly seemed so stupid that I had let my life be ruled by running and competing. I didn't need to live my life by such an extreme routine. It hadn't ever made me happy in a meaningful way. So what was the point in going back to it?

But ... although I didn't want to go back to my old routine, I couldn't escape the feeling that the more physically able I felt, the more fidgety I became. I knew my body was craving something active to do. I didn't want to lose control again, and this time, I knew I needed some professional help.

I looked for someone specialising in sports and mental health; someone who could empathise with what I'd been through. Scrolling through the options, I was excited to find a sports therapist called Rebecca, who focused on working with professional and amateur sportspeople suffering from performance anxiety and other psychological issues.

Rebecca was easy to talk to, and it was a huge relief to be able to tell my whole story to someone impartial. We clicked straight away. She told me that she had gone through something similar herself, and that made things so much easier. For the first time, I was really able to connect with someone who understood my struggles.

The fact that she was a sportswoman herself, and had clients in the same position as me, was reassuring – it meant I wasn't the only one facing those problems.

Rebecca gave me bespoke exercise and nutrition plans to follow to help me manage my emotions and exercise, so that I didn't go back to my old, extreme, regime. It was comforting to hear her say that I could take up running again and not go completely cold turkey. I was surprised at how different her sensible exercise programme was to my previous one. The duration of the physical activity was reduced by half, and she included rest days, which I hadn't done in years. I had to learn not to push myself too much, and accept that a harder lesson, like going for a long run wouldn't always solve my problems.

The key aspect of the therapy was communication. In the past, I had suppressed my feelings to protect myself and not hurt or upset others. But she emphasised how important it was to chat to my family and keep them included in my life. She said that if I was more open to them, they would be more understanding. They might even be able to help me overcome my anxieties or stress so that I didn't feel like I had to numb my suffering through running. By bottling up my emotions, like I had in the past, I had excluded myself from my family, without ever really meaning to. That's why my relationship with Mum had broken down.

Deep down, I knew Rebecca was right. I didn't want to lose Mum's love again. Since coming out of hospital our relationship had been much better, because I had started to change, and she could see the improvements.

I had come so far, and my relationships with Mum and Natalie had started to mend. I didn't want to lose them again. It was time to show them that I could overcome my obsession with running, and be their loving daughter and sister again.

I couldn't wait to tie up my running shoe laces a few days later. I felt ready. I deliberately didn't wear my watch, so that I wasn't tempted to time myself. The main aim of going for a "slow jog" was to clear my head and relax. I didn't need to go for hours of gruelling hill sprints and high mileage. It was far more beneficial to simply go out for a short run and not worry about time and distance.

I had become so accustomed to hitting my weekly targets that the new approach felt so refreshing by comparison. I was a little breathless at first, and my muscles were stiff, but after 10 minutes my body loosened up and I felt the same feelings of elation, even though I didn't go out for long. Maybe just half an hour, but it was enough. I was upbeat and energised when I returned, chuffed that my new attitude to running had paid off.

Not every run was as short or easy, and there were times when I had a bit of an internal battle maintaining my new routine. There were days when I would go for a long run or cycle just because I was "in the moment" and didn't want to stop. It was hard to resist the urge to do more than my therapist advised. I expressed my concerns with Rebecca and she reassured me, saying it was completely normal, and that I shouldn't feel guilty if I exceeded her guidelines. The best thing to do was to get back on track the next day and include more rest to allow my body to recuperate.

She reminded me that my goal was to get back to feeling fit and to re-learn how to enjoy running. It wasn't necessary to do strenuous activities every day. My body wasn't invincible. We only had to look at the injuries and my complete collapse to know that! I had abused myself by running such ludicrous distances in the past. It was time to establish a better balance in my life so that I didn't automatically opt for exercise to cope with negative feelings.

As I had more time available to enrich my life in other ways, I took up a number of hobbies. I finally learnt how to horse ride properly. Ever since my 9th birthday horse-riding party, I had dreamt of having regular lessons, but it had been too expensive for my parents. Now seemed the perfect opportunity to make it a reality ...

I used some of my savings to buy some riding gear and booked a series of lessons at my local riding centre. As soon as I stepped out of the car and walked into the paddock I was tingling with excitement.I hadn't ridden in years, but within minutes of being mounted on a gentle chestnut horse called Elsie, I was happily trotting along as if I I'd been riding all my life. My instructor, Danni, was fantastic, very calm and positive as she reminded me of the basics, and assessed my ability. I didn't want the lesson to end. I was comfortable in the saddle and felt at ease stroking Elsie's mane as we cantered around the arena.

I forgot about everything else going on in my life and solely concentrated on Danni's instructions, and the motion of being on horseback. I felt invigorated and had a rush of adrenaline as I swung my leg round to get off and take Elsie back to her stable. I offered to untack and groom her afterwards too. I nattered away to Elsie as I combed her tail. I didn't realise how therapeutic being around horses could be; they are such magnificently strong and serene animals.

I'm still continuing to ride now, and I've progressed to jumping and performing dressage routines. When I'm riding, I feel at one with nature as we canter along; we are a team. Every time she leaps over a fence I feel exhilarated and want to do it again. I've been on a few Sunday morning hacks as well in Windsor Great Park, and feel as if all my troubles dissolve, so that, by the end, I feel calm and capable of overcoming any of life's challenges.

I feel most proud and happy though when Mum comes to watch me ride. Even though she is allergic to horse hair, she still insists on accompanying me to my dressage competitions. Seeing her waving in the audience brings back the same emotions I had when I was Bluebird in Snow White when I was five. As soon as I ride into the arena for my performance I have butterflies in my stomach and can't wait to begin. Obviously, I want to win the coveted red rosette, but even when I don't, I still get that sense of elation that Mum is there sharing the experience with me.

There are times of course when I can't just drive to the stables and go horse riding when I feel stressed or upset. Rebecca suggested incorporating some other, less physical, home-based activities into my routine.

I remembered Dad in the hospice, and thought of how much joy he'd got from art. I had always loved drawing when I was growing up, and one afternoon, I brought down all my school art folders and sketch pads from the top of the wardrobe. Leafing through them made me glow with pride as the memories came flooding back to me. I had forgotten the simple pleasure of doing a pencil or biro drawing and decided to get back into the habit of drawing pictures every week. Sitting at the kitchen table with my old art pencils sprawled out in front of me was brilliant. I would get completely absorbed in my drawing for ages. Finishing every new picture gave me a real sense of accomplishment and I would feel my mood lighten.

Why hadn't I continued embracing art sooner? It was the perfect antidote for stress, and now I've gone on to make special occasion cards for friends and family, just like Dad used to. I love carrying on that tradition, just as I loved getting those cards from Dad. And now I hope it shows how much I care for the person I give every card to.

When I feel the stress levels rising, or I feel the urge to let off steam, I usually go for a walk outside, rather than going for a run like I used to. Engaging with nature has always been so therapeutic for me, so I began volunteering with my local parks and recreation team. I signed up for the weekly butterfly and deer surveys – which makes my rambles in the woods and parks more meaningful. I love the feeling that I'm doing something that contributes to my local area. I've also made new friends while out and about. Being in the company of other like-minded people enjoying nature never fails to brighten my day.

I no longer live a one-dimensional life of running to the exclusion of everything else. I'm evolving much more as a person, so that I'm always trying to embrace new opportunities, and meet new people. I feel more relaxed and comfortable with my new identity.

Mum has noticed the difference. She knows what I've been through, so when she compliments me on the journey I've made – with such love in her voice – it fills my heart with joy. She didn't nag me about over-exerting myself, and she didn't interrogate me about my discussions with Rebecca. She gave me the space I needed to develop and make the changes in my own time. She could see I was making progress, and she made the effort to spend time with me to support me. We started doing more things together too – so we'll go shopping in town, or spend a day in London going for a Dim Sum, just like we used to.

As we chat and engage in each's other lives more, our relationship has continued to get better. I've started to work for Mum part-time, to help with her business, and working as a team has been really good for us. I think that for her, being able to share some of the stresses and strains of running her own business with me really helped.

By the summer of 2016, I was in a much better place mentally and physically. Rebecca agreed that there wasn't much more she could do, except to let me continue by myself and see how I get on. I wasn't nervous about stopping my therapy with her because I was confident in myself and had changed my approach to life.

Mum and I booked a long weekend away together to celebrate. Not even gale-force winds could spoil our time on our trip to the island of Jersey. We spent the days exploring the island's exquisite beaches and indulging in the abundant seafood. It made me realise how much I had missed our family holidays, and it was great to be able to make some new memories together.

Gradually over the months I feel a transformation has taken place. I'm slowly emerging from my cocoon and blossoming into a butterfly. I don't feel the need to have a strict exercise regime to feel happy or secure; I have other ways of coping with life's pressures.

There are occasions when I still miss Dad immeasurably, and sometimes, for no apparent reason, I feel teary, and wish again that he were still alive. But that doesn't mean I'm still grieving for him. I try to remind myself that although he is not physically here, he will always be with me in my heart. I've come to accept the fact that I don't have to do anything "for him" to make him proud. I'm freer to live my life how I want, without feeling guilty now. This includes going for runs – not because I have to, but because I feel like it.

Running has become something I look forward to again. I'm not pressurising myself to follow a strict plan like I used to. I don't feel guilty when I don't go as far as I've aimed for. Now, I decide if I'm in the mood for a run when I get up in the morning. If the weather is appalling, or I'm just too tired, then I don't go. I know there's no point in risking getting injured by running in poor weather or through overtraining. Instead I'll choose to do something else that's just as personally rewarding.

This means that, when I do go for my runs, I feel refreshed and energised by them. As soon as my trainers touch the soft woodland floor, all my senses become alive. My shoulders drop as the tension from my body melts away, and I breathe in deeply, soaking up the nature all around me. I've run in the woods so many times, I feel as if I could run the route with my eyes shut. My feet know where to go, so the rest of me tunes directly into the surrounding sights and smells.

I love running in all the seasons because that's what makes running so interesting and unique – no two runs are the same. I notice the tiniest of changes, such as the first bluebells and primroses popping up in spring, which makes me smile. One of my favourite times to head out for a run is when it's just rained; the atmosphere is cool, the blackbirds start singing again, and the water-droplets evaporate off the trees and flowers creating a magical mist.

Now, each time I head out for a run, the time passes very quickly. It doesn't take long before I'm content with my loop around the woods, and then I head home in high spirits. I try to make a mental note of all the wildlife I've seen, but I've usually lost count of the number of robins I've spotted. It feels like they're always with me, fluttering beside me as I run by. In a way I feel like a robin while I run because I feel so happy, free and curious about what's happening around me.

I realise now that running will always be a part of me. I was born to run, just like Dad. It's an integral part of who I am, but I'm no longer defined by it. I'm not "just a runner" because now I've added so many more strings to my bow.

I used to think that running further and further gave me a greater sense of value and worth. But as time has gone on, I've learnt that isn't true. It was never true. It is true that I feel euphoric after a run, or any exercise; but I know that the release of endorphins won't paper over wounds that I need to heal in other ways.

Life isn't perfect, and I can't control everything that happens, which can still make me feel uneasy at times. But, rather than resorting to exercise to escape feeling anxious and stressed, I know there are other more effective ways to cope with these situations. I have my family and friends to talk to. And I have other ways to deal with the difficult things now.

I know who I am, and I know who I want to be. I respect myself more, and I spend time doing more important things with my life. I think I've found a far more rewarding way to live.

Most importantly I've discovered that I can conquer my fears. As a little girl, I was terrified of losing Mum or Dad. I couldn't imagine ever being happy again without either of them in my life. When Dad died, I was completely distraught. Just like Simba in *The Lion King*, I felt lost; incomplete. I lived as if I was constantly "searching" for him, desperate to be with him again. I didn't know any other way to live.

I was constantly striving to prove my worth – to show that I wasn't a failure; that I was strong. It was my way of surviving. Running had been my crutch – something to comfort me and fill the enormous void in my life after Dad's death. But my collapse changed all that. It made me look at life differently. Gradually, I learnt how to be less harsh on myself, and in time, I came to accept that I didn't need to live my life for Dad. Mum reminded me that Dad loved me for who I was, no matter what, just like she does. All she wants is for me to be happy in life. I don't need to feel guilty if I don't win or finish top; all I can do is my best.

Nothing and no one will ever replace Dad. But as the years have gone by, I have learnt how to live without him. Rather than just seeing the loss of Dad as a tragedy, I can see the positives that have come about, as I have come to terms with it. I've become more resilient and independent, and I've achieved things I never even dreamt I could do, from horse riding to competing in the London Marathon. Not having Dad around has inspired me to tackle challenges and overcome them; to do things I wouldn't have done if he had still been with us. It's not been easy, but I have grown so much over the last few years, mentally and emotionally. I'm proud of how my family and I have supported each other along this journey.

I'm more conscious of how precious life is now. I understand what truly matters. For me, that is spending time doing the things I love with the people I care about the most. Mum and Natalie mean the world to me; they've been with me every step of the way, and I'm at my happiest when we're all together.

I still feel such a deep connection to my dad. Whenever I visit his grave, my thoughts go back to the times we shared, and my love for him will never fade. Best of all, I've got all his camcorder videos. Whenever I want to hear his voice and laugh at the people we were, I put one on and revel in the memories. Dad may not be here in the flesh, but he will live on in my memories, and in my heart.

If you found this book interesting ...
why not read this next?

Body Image Problems
& Body Dysmorphic Disorder

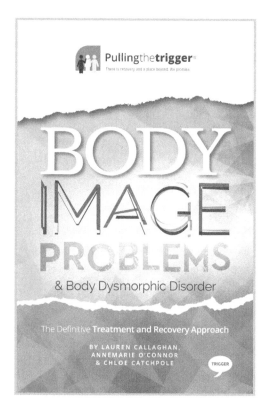

This unique and inspiring book provides simple yet highly effective self-help methods to help you overcome your body image concerns and Body Dysmorphic Disorder (BDD).

If you found this book interesting ...
why not read this next?

Stand Tall Little Girl

Facing up to Anorexia

Stand Tall Little Girl shares the harrowing, yet truly inspiring, journey of a girl that fought from rock bottom to beat her 'friend' Anorexia.

the *Shaw* mind
FOUNDATION

Creating hope for children,
adults and families

Sign up to our charity, The Shaw Mind Foundation
www.shawmindfoundation.org
and keep in touch with us; we would love to hear
from you.

*We aim to bring to an end the suffering and despair caused
by mental health issues. Our goal is to make help and support
available for every single person in society, from all walks of
life. We will never stop offering hope. These are our promises.*

www.triggerpublishing.com

Trigger is a publishing house devoted to opening conversations about mental health. We tell the stories of people who have suffered from mental illnesses and recovered, so that others may learn from them.

Adam Shaw is a worldwide mental health advocate and philanthropist. Now in recovery from mental health issues, he is committed to helping others suffering from debilitating mental health issues through the global charity he co-founded, The Shaw Mind Foundation. www.shawmindfoundation.org

Lauren Callaghan (CPsychol, PGDipClinPsych, PgCert, MA (hons), LLB (hons), BA), born and educated in New Zealand, is an innovative industry-leading psychologist based in London, United Kingdom. Lauren has worked with children and young people, and their families, in a number of clinical settings providing evidence based treatments for a range of illnesses, including anxiety and obsessional problems. She was a psychologist at the specialist national treatment centres for severe obsessional problems in the UK and is renowned as an expert in the field of mental health, recognised for diagnosing and successfully treating OCD and anxiety related illnesses in particular. In addition to appearing as a treating clinician in the critically acclaimed and BAFTA award-winning documentary *Bedlam*, Lauren is a frequent guest speaker on mental health conditions in the media and at academic conferences. Lauren also acts as a guest lecturer and honorary researcher at the Institute of Psychiatry Kings College, UCL.

Please visit the link below:

www.triggerpublishing.com

Join us and follow us...

@triggerpub

Search for us on Facebook